NINETEENTH-CENTURY AMERICAN WOMEN THEATRE MANAGERS

D0169047

NINETEENTH-CENTURY AMERICAN WOMEN THEATRE MANAGERS

Jane Kathleen Curry

Contributions in Women's Studies, Number 143

GREENWOOD PRESS
Westport, Connecticut • London

Library of Congress Cataloging-in-Publication Data

Curry, Jane Kathleen.
    Nineteenth-century American women theatre managers / Jane Kathleen
Curry.
        p.   cm.—(Contributions in women's studies, ISSN 0147–104X ;
no. 143)
    Includes bibliographical references and index.
    ISBN 0–313–29141–1 (alk. paper)
    1. Theater management—United States—History—19th century.
2. Women in the theater—United States—History—19th century.
3. Theatrical managers—United States—Biography. 4. Women
theatrical managers—United States—Biography. I. Title.
II. Series.
PN2291.C87   1994
792′.023′082—dc20   93–44133

British Library Cataloguing in Publication Data is available.

792.023
C976n
1994

Library of Congress Catalog Card Number: 93–44133
ISBN: 0–313–29141–1
ISSN: 0147–104X

First published in 1994

Greenwood Press, 88 Post Road West, Westport, CT 06881
An imprint of Greenwood Publishing Group, Inc.

Printed in the United States of America

The paper used in this book complies with the
Permanent Paper Standard issued by the National
Information Standards Organization (Z39.48–1984).

10 9 8 7 6 5 4 3 2

For my parents, Barbara and Richard Curry

Contents

Acknowledgments

I would like to take this opportunity to thank my former teachers, especially those who had a direct impact on this project: R. B. Graves, Don B. Wilmeth, Walter J. Meserve, Judith Milhous, and Marvin Carlson.

I would also like to mention just a few of the many people who deserve thanks for providing assistance and encouragement. The short list includes Kathleen Morgan, Vera Mowry Roberts, Jan Heissinger, Eileen Berkon, Jack Hrkach, Paula Longo, Emily Hegarty, Danielle Mead, Edward Dee, Joel Berkowitz, Shauna Vey, David Roll, Robert Grenier, Doug Giebel, Joanna Kurtz, Joel K. Soiseth, Chris Curry, Molly Curry, and Richard Medoff.

Introduction

"I know of no other vocation except literature in which a woman stands on a footing of absolute equality with a man. If an actress is capable of doing as good work as an actor she receives the same remuneration that he does," observed stage star Kate Claxton in 1894.[1] Seeing their opportunity, thousands of women throughout the nineteenth century turned to the theatre in the United States for a basic living and with a hope of gaining the reputation necessary for demanding a large weekly salary. More remarkably, a few determined women took full advantage of the unique career path available in the theatre to assume the important position of theatre manager. The various responsibilities of a theatre manager were likely to include managing a stock company, owning or leasing a theatre, hiring actors and other personnel, selecting plays for production, directing rehearsals, supervising all production details, and promoting the pieces offered to the public. Having included women at every level of skill and responsibility from its first appearance in America, the professional English-language theatre provided an unusual occupational field. The managerial roles held by women in the theatre are especially significant in their frequent contrast to evolving standards of proper and acceptable work for women.

Since the earliest colonial days white women have worked in America. The difficulty of life in the New World meant that the labor of all hands was necessary for family and community survival. At first, most basic needs, such as food, clothing, and furniture, were met by home production, and when specialization of labor did occur it was not unusual for all members of a family to participate in the enterprise. In the colonial period widows, especially those who did not hastily remarry, frequently assumed the trade of their deceased husbands, working, for example, as printers or merchants. This was possible because the women had been involved in the day-to-day operations of their husbands' trade and possessed the required knowledge and skill. Other widows used their inherited property, typically the family home, to launch an enterprise such as an inn or school.   Local communities usually encouraged the industrious widows, who often provided some needed service while relieving the community of the potential burden of supporting them and their families.[2]

Increased urbanization and industrialization at the end of the eighteenth century and especially at the beginning of the nineteenth century led to a decline in family production and moved much work out of the home, taking with it most men.   Division of labor along gender lines became more formalized, with women's work increasingly devalued and women isolated in their homes. After a husband's death, for example, a woman could no longer be expected to continue his business, as she was usually not well acquainted with his work. Instead of working alongside their husbands, married women were encouraged to concentrate on child rearing and creating comfortable, well-regulated homes. Some women, of course, remained in the work force, but most of these were found in lower-class jobs, performing either low-status women's work, such as domestic service, or unskilled factory labor, where they received lower wages than men even for identical work, along with constant resentment for the threat they posed to men's employment. Called working girls, the women employed in these ill-paid, monotonous jobs with little chance for advancement were usually young, single, and expecting to remain in the work force for only a few years before marriage. Great pressure was placed on married women to remain at home, using their superior moral sense to influence their husbands and to guide the formation of their children's characters, rather than risking their virtue in a harsh workplace. Further, with widespread accumulation of wealth in the new country, the presence of a wife in the home took on an element of conspicuous display, demonstrating the wage-earning ability of the male breadwinner. Rather than break the social prohibition against married women's employment, poor families often sent children to work and encouraged the wife to supplement the family income at home by taking in boarders or sewing piecework. A widow with small children who wished to remain at home might barely survive by doing the same poorly paid piecework. Even a single woman working outside the home to support other family members had difficulty earning an adequate income under a system which assumed that only men might have dependents.[3]

Women from more prosperous families created the domestic ideal which defined women's sphere of activity throughout the nineteenth century. Neither wealthy women, whose only responsibility was to oversee the household servants, nor middle-class women, who did not work outside the home but often had to perform all the strenuous though little appreciated housework themselves, contributed directly to their families' financial well-being. Instead, they developed a role for themselves as the emotional center of the family, providing comfort and a proper moral influence. Higher status women's jobs, positions that usually required some education and would not prevent a young woman so employed from eventually making a good marriage, included social work, nursing, and teaching, all occupations that could be seen as an extension of women's "natural" role in the home.[4]   Of course, not all women performing privileged domestic roles were content.   Women in teaching and other good women's jobs had few career options and were not paid well in comparison to men of similar family background and educational level.   Also many bored and isolated, wealthy women with extra time on their hands, joined by middle-class women as technology relieved much of the burden of housework, began to look for fulfillment beyond their own parlors.

Because of many women's dissatisfaction in work or domestic roles, the struggle to define the proper role for women in society was a concern throughout the nineteenth century.   Many women worked to expand the traditional definitions of womanhood, encouraging women to take part in philanthropic or reform activities.   They also urged higher education for women, usually on the grounds that this would make them better mothers and wives, with the result that the number of women teachers increased dramatically.   More radical feminists supported the efforts of women to hold traditionally male, high-status jobs—for example, as doctors, lawyers, or ministers—and helped other groups of women, such as garment workers and shop girls, organize for better working conditions and wages.   Besides the issues of fair compensation and fewer restrictions on career opportunities, feminists in the second half of the nineteenth century were concerned with issues such as full suffrage for women and reform in married women's property laws.[5]   Often collectively referred to as the "woman question," these controversial ideas were continually debated as many women sought to expand their participation in the public realm.

It is useful to consider women theatre managers in light of both the jobs typically performed by working women and the more rewarding careers that a small number of women were struggling to achieve later in the nineteenth century.   Women found unique career opportunities in the theatre, but at times, like women in other male-dominated fields, women theatre managers faced difficulties due to gender.   Challenging the pressure to conform to ideals of womanly behavior operating in the larger society, women assumed positions of leadership within the theatre.   By observing the ambitions, obstacles, and successes of the highly visible women theatre managers, it is possible to learn more not only about the theatre, but also about the expectations, restrictions, and possibilities for women, both as a group and as exceptional individuals, throughout the nineteenth century.

Unlike many other occupations, the theatre attracted women from every type of background.   That the field provided strong employment prospects for women, most commonly as actresses, means the theatre should not be overlooked in studying women's employment throughout the nineteenth century.   Of course, many women, especially early in the century, entered the theatrical profession by being born into it.   Mrs. John Drew is the classic example of this type, as her career of nearly eighty years, including thirty years as a manager, began when her mother carried her onstage as an infant.

For many working-class women entering the theatre, even as a "ballet girl," meant relatively good wages and working conditions compared to other options, such as domestic service. There was also the possibility to work up in the profession or, once on the stage, to attract the attention of a wealthy man and marry into a higher social class. Of course, women usually left the theatre if they married outside the profession. Middle-class women, widows and especially daughters, facing difficult times sometimes turned to the stage, where education, refined speech, and graceful manners could help some of them succeed. Even the wealthiest and most socially prominent women in this country were sometimes attracted to the stage. Beautiful society women who could pay for their own stage debuts usually started in leading roles, rarely training in lesser parts and rarely earning much acclaim or staying long in the theatre. However, there were exceptions, such as Lily Langtry, who had a highly successful career.

Early in the nineteenth century several women assumed theatre management positions, usually more through necessity than ambition. Some women inherited a theatre following the death of a husband and continued to manage because of a sense of familial obligation or responsibility for an already established company. Mrs. Anne Brunton Merry Wignell Warren, for example, took on a managerial role following the death of her husband, Thomas Wignell, in February 1803. Other women turned to management in order to provide themselves with a performance venue when their other options were limited. Elizabeth Hamblin, for example, opened her own theatre in New York City in 1836 following her divorce from theatre manager Thomas S. Hamblin, and Charlotte Baldwin, not satisfied with her compensation at the Park Theatre, opened the City Theatre under her own management in 1822.[6]

As all theatre practitioners in the early nineteenth century lived and worked somewhat outside of the boundaries of respectable society, they tended to allow a greater flexibility in defining women's work, with less concern for socially enforced restrictions on behavior. In the theatre women were not denied training and entry-level employment as they were in many other fields. Working as an actress, a woman had plenty of opportunity to observe theatre managers at work and to prepare for a management career essentially the same way a man would. Some women, including Mrs. John Drew, Frances Anne Denny Drake, and Miss A. G. Trimble, also had the advantage of observing at close range the management of husbands or fathers before becoming managers themselves. This relative ease of entry to the profession was in sharp contrast to the experience of the would-be woman doctor, for example, to whom many medical schools were closed until well into the twentieth century. The first woman to earn a regular medical degree in the United States, Elizabeth Blackwell, only gained admission to Geneva College, a less-than-prestigious medical school, after the student body voted her in as a joke. Completing her degree along with postgraduate training in Europe, Dr. Blackwell was forced to buy a building in order to start her practice because she was unable to convince anyone in New York City to rent rooms to her.[7]

Besides having adequate training, a woman who worked in the theatre was not as likely as her nontheatrical counterpart to have qualms about the business aspect of theatre management. Commerce was clearly defined as a male enterprise in nineteenth-century America and considered dangerous to a woman's character and respectability. Since women in theatre had already challenged notions of respectability when they entered the profession, they were probably less likely to have their managerial ambitions checked by social pressure.

One major problem facing women in theatre management that did not deter pioneer career women in other fields was the theatre managers' dependence on pleasing a large public. Women doctors and lawyers could survive with the support of ardent feminists and practice on charity cases even if the rest of the world laughed. Women in theatre needed widespread approval for their endeavors. As most women managers were also actresses whose popularity and income depended on their presentation of idealized feminine qualities through various characters, a woman had to take care that her assumption of the powerful, male-identified position of manager did not undermine her public persona. The paradoxical position of the nineteenth-century actress in light of dominant social behavior has been examined by Tracy Davis in a study of English actresses, which points out that while the actress was admired for portraying a womanly ideal, the actual behavior of the actress—pursuing a career, displaying her personal beauty for a profit—was in opposition to social norms.[8] Women theatre managers further challenged social norms by operating businesses and employing and supervising other women and men. Yet, while their mere existence could be read as a threat to the social order, most women managers were careful not to disturb the status quo more than necessary. They presented themselves not as part of a large-scale movement to change socially controlled gender roles, but as individual women who, through personal industry and artistic ability, were qualified to manage the public's entertainment.[9] While women theatre managers were highly visible examples of women holding responsible, powerful positions, providing a sign of hope for other ambitious women, they did not, for the most part, encourage other women to follow their example, and they could not afford to be outspoken advocates of feminist issues. Not until early in the twentieth century did equal suffrage for women, the most promoted feminist issue of the day, gather sufficient public interest for several prominent theatre women, for example Mary Shaw, to risk becoming active supporters of the cause.[10]

Beyond subtle, psychological pressure on actresses not to disturb the status quo in assuming managerial duties, women managers sometimes encountered direct opposition. Occasionally, men in the theatre, certainly aware of the wider culture's tendency to restrict women's employment opportunities, resented working for a woman or feared the additional competition provided by women as managerial rivals. Newspaper critics, who influenced the way in which the efforts of all managers were received by the public, also could present difficulties for women managers, though most often their negative commentary did not extend beyond condescension dressed up as praise for the "fair manageress" and her "pretty little theatre."[11] It is also necessary to remember that restrictions on married women's right to control their own property had the potential to make almost any business transaction legally impossible for a married woman manager. While exceptions to restrictive legislation seem to have been made for most women working as managers, it is possible that some women managers had to rely at times on the legal capacities of their business managers or other male employees. Many adjustments in married women's property laws were made over the years, complicating the situation for women and not always improving it. The confused situation made it hazardous for anyone to enter into a contract with a married woman, for often the courts found women not liable for their debts if their contracts were not made with a husband's knowledge and approval. Citing such precedents one theatre manager, Sarah Conway, during a period of financial difficulty, attempted to avoid paying her printer. However, the court found that as the recognized proprietor of a business, clearly named Mrs. Conway's Theatre, her signature was good, and she was liable for her own debts.[12] While Mrs. Conway presumably was disappointed to lose her case, the long-term effect for women was positive, for married women would succeed in business only if, like men and like single women, they could be expected to honor their contracts. In another case, though a judge eventually dismissed the objection, Laura Keene's right to bring suit in her effort to protect her rights to Tom Taylor's *Our American Cousin* was challenged by William Wheatley and John Sleeper Clarke on the grounds that she was married.[13]

This study finds that, by and large, absolute barriers to women's participation in the profession of theatrical management did not exist. Still, examination of individual cases reveals women maneuvering to balance the demands of management with an awareness of suitable gendered behavior. The patriarchal organization of nineteenth-century American society supported a pervasive ideology of restricted roles for women in the public sphere. Even as the definition of acceptable work roles for women advanced and shifted, the dominant ideology affected both the public postures assumed by women managers and the critical response to their efforts.

This account of women theatre managers in the United States during the nineteenth century includes a discussion of the managerial activities of more than fifty managers. Many of these women, among the most outstanding managers of their day, had productive careers that should be recorded, if only to negate the easy assumption that theatre managers were always men. Others were not especially successful, but are included here simply because they attempted to establish themselves as managers. This, in itself, is significant. Theatre management was a risky and difficult business even under the best of circumstances, but these women at least accepted the challenge and presumably thought they had a chance to succeed.

This book includes all the women who were important figures in theatre management, as well as some who were not widely known even in their own day. A few more women who would fit in the latter category undoubtedly remain to be rediscovered. The theatre managers discussed here worked in many parts of the country, though the greatest number were active in the major theatre cities of New York and Philadelphia. Detailed attention is not given in this work to women who managed traveling companies but did not attempt to establish a permanent residence in a particular theatre. While an impressive number of women headed theatre companies on the road, it is difficult to follow all their tracks about the country, and in many cases it is practically impossible to determine whether the woman actually managed the company or merely lent her name to a company in which she starred.[14]

The first chapter provides an account of the pioneers, fifteen women who, often out of necessity, became managers in various parts of the country and, for the most part, were unaware of being part of a larger trend of women in management. All of them were managing theatres before 24 December 1853, when Catherine Sinclair, often incorrectly cited as the first woman theatre manager in the United States, opened the Metropolitan Theatre in San Francisco.[15] Sinclair and four others who took advantage of the California Gold Rush to launch managerial careers are discussed in the second chapter. One of those women, Laura Keene, went on to achieve prominence as a manager in New York City. She is the focus of the next chapter. As the first woman to establish herself as manager of a large, first-class house in New York, Keene attracted a great deal of attention and even direct opposition to her management. Her career provides good examples of both the frustrations and satisfactions encountered by women theatre managers. The fourth chapter deals with another outstanding woman manager, Louisa Lane Drew, along with three other Philadelphia managers. Chapter five examines the careers of more than fifteen New Yorkers and Brooklynites[16] who entered theatre management after Laura Keene, most notably Mrs. John Wood and Sarah Conway. Ten women who managed theatres in other parts of the country during the second half of the nineteenth century are the subject of a final chapter before the conclusion.

No full examination of the many nineteenth-century American women who undertook theatre management has been completed, despite the fact that a handful of individual women are featured in full-length studies. As a result the few outstanding managers to receive scholarly attention are often treated as isolated anomalies, rather than considered within the context of a historical period which included a number of women managers. In order to correct the impression that theatres managed by women were extremely rare, this book includes information on more than fifty women managers, most of whom have been overlooked by recent scholars. Clearly, a fuller appreciation of the achievements of the best-known managers, Keene and Drew, is possible when their careers are discussed in conjunction with less familiar names, such as Sarah Kirby Stark, Elizabeth Bowers, and Sarah Conway. New perspectives are presented as each manager is considered in relation to the others. The number of other women currently managing theatres, the precedent of women managers in a particular city, and attitudes about women managers expressed by critics were all factors affecting the career of any individual woman manager. Overall, this work attempts to document the fact that women, despite legal limitations and social restrictions, were regularly, actively, and in some instances successfully involved in theatre management throughout the century.

NOTES

1. *Dramatic Mirror*, 8 December 1894, 2.

2. For more information on the work of American women during the colonial period, see Elisabeth Anthony Dexter, *Colonial Women of Affairs before 1776* (1931; reprint, Clifton, N.J.: Augustus M. Kelley, 1972), and Julie A. Matthaei, "Women's Work in the Colonial Family Economy," in *An Economic History of Women in America: Women's Work, the Sexual Division of Labor, and the Development of Capitalism* (New York: Schocken Books, 1982).

3. Susan Estabrook Kennedy, "Part One: She Must be Married, Because She Don't Work," in *If All We Did Was to Weep at Home: A History of White Working-Class Women in America* (Bloomington: Indiana University Press, 1979), and Edith Abbott, *Women in Industry: A Study in American Economic History* (1910; reprint, New York: Arno Press and the New York Times, 1969).

4. Catherine Beecher, a strong advocate of women teachers in the 1820s and 1830s, correctly predicted that women would meet the demand for teachers during the country's western expansion while men turned to more lucrative occupations. Elisabeth Anthony Dexter, *Career Women of America 1776–1840* (1950; reprint, Clifton, N.J.: Augustus M. Kelley, 1972), 23–25.

5. In New York, for example, married women did not gain the legal right to make contracts until 1884 and were not guaranteed sole and separate right to their own wages until 1902. See Peggy A. Rabkin, *Fathers to Daughters: The Legal Foundations of Female Emancipation* (Westport, Conn.: Greenwood Press, 1980).

6. George C. D. Odell, *Annals of the New York Stage* (New York: Columbia University Press, 1927–41; New York: AMS Press, 1970), 3:33, 4:102–3.

7. H. J. Mozans, *Woman in Science* (1913; reprint, Cambridge: MIT Press, 1974), 300–303. For more on barriers encountered by women in

medicine see Mary Roth Walsh, *"Doctors Wanted: No Women Need Apply"*: *Sexual Barriers in the Medical Profession, 1835-1975* (New Haven: Yale University Press, 1977).

8. Tracy Davis, "Actresses and Prostitutes in Victorian London," *Theatre Research International* 13 (Autumn 1988): 220-34.

9. American women managers of the nineteenth century did not choose to produce drama that was overtly feminist or that differed radically from that presented by their male counterparts, and like the men they continued to place conventional images of women on the stage.   Laura Keene, for example, adorned her stage with beautiful women to help draw crowds to her spectacular pieces, which can be seen as precursors to *The Black Crook* and other "leg dramas."

10. Albert Auster, *Actresses and Suffragists: Women in the American Theatre 1890-1920* (New York: Praeger, 1984).

11. Laura Keene as a woman manager seems to have been singled out to receive the greatest critical opposition on the grounds of gender. This was due in part to the high profile of her management, at a large, first-class theatre in New York City, and to the fact that she appeared to manage out of ambition rather than necessity and did not inherit her managerial position from a husband or father. Also she was the first of a wave of women managers to work in that city during the second half of the nineteenth-century.

Of course, Keene received many positive notices in the press, but this praise was frequently diminished by comments on the prettiness and diminutiveness (even though not literally true) of her theatre. For example, her theatre is called a "pretty little house" in the *Spirit of the Times* (10 January 1857) and a "bijou of a theatre" in the *New York Herald* (4 February 1857). (Her plays, as well as the theatre, were called "nice, little" and "pretty" in a number of examples in the *Herald* during March 1857.)   Almost every woman manager to receive significant press coverage was given some "pretty little" praise. In the *Spirit of the Times* Mrs. John Wood's theatre was called a "pretty house" (17 December 1864), Lina Edwin's theatre called a "pretty theatre" (24 December 1870), and Madame de Marguerittes's theatre called a "nice little theatre" (5 February 1853).

Even a woman manager's physical stature was apt to be made small through idiomatic slurs in the press. Keene was described in the *Spirit of the Times* as a "brave little woman" (14 March 1857) and as "that dear little body of a directress" on (30 May 1857).   Women managers were regularly described in terms which reminded readers that they were not just managers, but also female. Mrs. John Drew was referred to as "the fair lessee" in the *Philadelphia Inquirer* (23 September 1861) and Lina Edwin was a "fair manageress" in the *Brooklyn Daily Eagle*, (14 November 1870).   Francis Courtney Wemyss, in *Twenty-Six Years in the Life of an Actor and Manager* (New York: Burgess, Stringer and Company, 1847), described Mary Elizabeth Maywood's management as a "petticoat government."   Women managers also received praise for any traditional feminine virtues they were believed to possess. After Keene cleaned her theatre for the start of a new season, the *Spirit of the Times* observed, "For clean rooms, houses, and hearths, there must be a woman 'to the fore'" (5 September 1857). Sarah Conway was praised by the *Brooklyn Daily Eagle* (26 April 1875) as "a good wife and a good mother."

12. Norma Basch, *In the Eyes of the Law: Women, Marriage and Property in Nineteenth-Century New York* (Ithaca: Cornell University Press, 1982), 211.

13. "Case No. 7644, Keene v. Wheatley et al.," in *The Federal Cases: Circuit and District Courts of the United States* (St. Paul: West Publishing Company, 1895), 14:191.

14. While examples of women managing touring companies can be found throughout the century, they are much more numerous after the 1860s, as the popularity of touring combination companies increased. For example, at least fifteen companies headed by women are mentioned in the *Spirit of the Times* between 1 November 1873 and 18 July 1874.

15. For example, see the entry on Laura Keene's Theatre by James Burge in Weldon B. Durham, ed., *American Theatre Companies, 1749–1887* (New York: Greenwood Press, 1986), 290. Burge states that Keene, opening the Howard Athenaeum in Baltimore on 23 December 1853, shares Sinclair's record as the "first theatrical manageress of record in America."

16. Brooklyn was a separate city from New York until 1898.

1

The Pioneers—Early Nineteenth-Century Women Theatre Managers in the United States

At least fourteen women managed theatres in the United States before Catherine Sinclair, Laura Keene, and Louisa Lane Drew attracted public attention to the phenomenon; however, the managements of these pioneers have been largely forgotten. Many of the early women managers were dependent on the theatre for their livelihood and opened their own theatre or assumed management either when a husband died or when a city's existing theatres did not provide them with adequate employment opportunities. Generally producing a short season or seasons for about a year, these women had managerial careers of respectable duration, given the difficulty of establishing a permanent theatre anywhere, in early nineteenth-century America, especially as a rival to an already operating theatre. Even in the biggest cities, only limited audiences were available during the early 1800s, and as the century progressed many of the women attempting management were in smaller, more remote cities, which presented the same problem of a restricted potential audience.

In addition to the remaining puritanical resistance to theatrical entertainment, managers had to face the mundane matter of a local audience becoming bored with a small troupe of regular players and preferring the novelty of new faces, which made long-term survival in one place quite difficult. It should also be remembered that most women managers of this period had acting, not managing, as their main goal, and managed a theatre only when necessary or expedient. The short duration of the managerial career of an actress who eventually accepted a more secure position with another manager, therefore, can often be viewed as an advance in an acting career, rather than a failure in management.

MARGARETTA SULLY WEST

The earliest women managers in the United States, Margaretta Sully West and Anne Brunton Merry, were actresses married to theatre managers, and both assumed managerial responsibilities when their husbands died. Margaretta Sully was married to Thomas Wade West, who left London to form a touring company in Virginia in 1790 with his son-in-law (or brother-in-law) John Bignall. The company had to travel in order to find sufficient audiences but was associated with permanent theatres, five of them built by Thomas West, in Richmond, Norfolk, Alexandria, Fredericksburg, and Petersburg, Virginia, and Charleston, South Carolina.[1] When Bignall died in 1794, his widow, Ann West Bignall, inherited a proprietary interest in the company but did not assume a managerial role. Margaretta Sully West became not only proprietor but manager of the company when Thomas West died in 1799. At first she was challenged by men who left her company to form their own managements, but within a couple of months these rival companies went out of existence.[2] Margaretta Sully West, who was named as the owner of the Norfolk Theatre even before the death of her husband, also supervised the construction of the Richmond Theatre, completed in 1806. During her management West relied on the repertory the company had developed under her husband's direction but also added some new pieces including a few written by Americans. For example, she produced *Liberty in Louisiana* by a citizen of Charleston and James Nelson Barker's *The Indian Princess*.[3] Although West gradually shifted many of the responsibilities of management to company member J. W. Green and appeared less frequently as an actress, she remained proprietor through the company's last recorded performances in 1809.[4]

ANNE BRUNTON MERRY WIGNELL WARREN

Anne Brunton Merry and her husband, Robert Merry, began their American acting careers in 1796. Having made her stage debut at the Theatre Royal, Bath, in 1785 at age sixteen, Mrs. Merry was an experienced actress who quickly became a star in the new country. After her husband died in 1798 and her contract to manager Thomas Wignell expired, Mrs. Merry considered returning to England or accepting an engagement with William Dunlap at the Park Theatre, New York. Ultimately she decided to renew her contract with Wignell and continue performing with his Philadelphia-based Chestnut Street Theatre Company. Making another sort of contract, she married Wignell on 1 January 1803, but unfortunately, on 21 February 1803, he died and Anne Merry Wignell suddenly became a manager. Though Mrs. Wignell left the stage for two months, the Chestnut Street Theatre was announced to continue under the management of Mrs. Wignell and Alexander Reinagle, Thomas Wignell's comanager, with the assistance of William Warren and William

Wood.[5] Soon resuming her position as leading actress, Mrs. Wignell with
Mr. Reinagle renewed the lease on the Chestnut in May 1803 for $2,500 per
year. She shared in the managerial responsibilities and risks without making
any noticeable changes in the direction of the jointly managed company, which
continued to perform a familiar repertory.

After a time management became a burden for the busy actress, who was
also a well-respected member of the community. Charles Durang noted:
''Mrs. Wignell had been a good deal annoyed in the business of the theatre;
some of the actors pressed their affairs with ungentleness. The conduct of a
company where a variety of dispositions are to be met, jealousies are to soothe
and intrigues are to be counteracted, requires more to bear up against, than the
nerves of a sensitive, generous and confiding woman.''[6] Preferring to
concentrate on acting rather than the regular troubles of management, Wignell
on 3 April 1805 transferred her share in the lease to William Warren, whom
she married on 28 August 1806.[7] As leading actress and wife of one of the
managers she maintained an influential position in the company. Less than two
years later, on 28 June 1808, Mrs. Warren died of complications from
childbirth. Having managed in partnership with men, Anne Wignell Warren
did not move the company in a clearly identifiable, independent direction.
While her place in the history of the American theatre is based primarily on
her contributions as an actress, her management was significant for
demonstrating that early in the nineteenth century in the United States a woman
could continue the managerial role of a deceased husband with at least partial
support from the company.

MRS. POWELL

Another widow and at least a theatre proprietor, Mrs. Snelling Powell
became lessee of a theatre, apparently managed by others, in Providence from
1817 for several years. The theatre had been leased in 1811 by Mr. Powell
and Mr. Dickson for five years. Mrs. Powell, who had been a popular actress
at the theatre, assumed the lease after the expiration of Powell and Dickson's
term.[8] Mrs. Powell also reportedly managed the Federal Street Theatre in
Boston with Thomas Kilner and Henry J. Finn.[9]

SARAH ROSS

The first woman theatrical manager in New York City was Miss Sarah
Ross at the Grove Theatre in 1804 according to Ruth Dimmick.[10] However,
George C. D. Odell (who places Frederick Wheatley, Ross's future husband,
at the scene) only acknowledged that Miss Ross acted with the Grove company,
first joining it in December 1804.[11] The management by Miss Ross would

be an interesting episode if true, especially as she became the mother of William Wheatley, the well-known manager.

CHARLOTTE BALDWIN

Next to appear on the managerial scene in New York City was a widow who did not inherit a theatre but instead established her own when her fortunes were down. Charlotte Baldwin, who played old women and comedy parts, came to the United States with her husband, Joseph, and made her debut at the Park Theatre in New York on 17 April 1816, playing the Nurse to the Juliet of her sister, Mrs. Mary Barnes. After the death of her husband and the destruction of the Park by fire on 24 May 1820, Baldwin was scheduled to receive a benefit at the Anthony Street Theatre, the new home of the Park company, on 26 June 1820, though it is not certain that this benefit actually took place. The next year Baldwin organized a benefit for herself at Washington Hall in which she was supported mostly by amateur gentlemen. This venture, held on 21 September 1821, apparently made some money and was repeated on a few more nights during the 1821–22 season, while Baldwin continued to perform at the Park. Encouraged by the success of these performances, she opened the City Theatre, a tiny theatre on the second floor of the building at 15 Warren Street on 2 July 1822. Odell reports that Baldwin left the Park company disgruntled by salary reductions and lack of benefits, and that by developing her benefit series into a more professional operation "shouted defiance to the men who had let her carry a grievance from the regular playhouse."[12] Certainly, in doing the ground work to open a new theatre by herself, rather than continuing the management of an established company, Baldwin demonstrated a new level of ambition on the part of women theatre managers in the United States.

The City Theatre remained in operation until 31 August 1822, when it was closed by a yellow fever scare, but it reopened 29 November 1822, and performances were held through 31 January 1823 and again from 17 February to 29 April. Among the plays Baldwin presented were *The Stranger*, *The School for Scandal*, *Jane Shore*, *The Mayor of Garratt*, *The Grecian Daughter*, *Fire and Water*, *The Heir at Law*, and *George Barnwell*, a mix of serious and comic standard English fare. Baldwin was briefly married to Mr. Westervelt Walstein, son of a New York merchant. He acted in some of her productions and may have had some role in the theatre's management, for on 2 April 1823 "[she] announced that the business of the Theatre would be *entirely* under her own management and on her own responsibility."[13] A final benefit to close the establishment was held on 13 June 1823. There is no further record of managerial activity on the part of Charlotte Baldwin, who retired from the stage in 1837 and died on 21 April 1856 at age 78.

ELIZABETH HAMBLIN

Thirteen years after Charlotte Baldwin's management three more New York women, Elizabeth Hamblin, Annette Nelson, and Virginia Monier, opened small theatres in quick succession. The most active manager of this group, Elizabeth Blanchard, had divorced the theatre manager Thomas S. Hamblin around 1834 but continued to use his name professionally.[14] Opening Mrs. Hamblin's Theatre at the Richmond Hill, a little used, five-year-old house at the corner of Varick and Charlton streets, on 13 June 1836, she produced a season that lasted through 11 August. Presenting plays such as *Luke the Labourer*, *The Wife*, and *No Song No Supper*, and a good deal of dance, including a ballet, *The Cobblers of Cobblestown*, Elizabeth Hamblin's company was reinforced by actors from the Franklin Theatre when it closed for the season in July.[15] Another short season managed by Mr. Charles and Mr. Teller and featuring Elizabeth Hamblin was produced from 27 August until 19 September 1836.[16] The Richmond Hill then became Miss Nelson's Theatre for a time, but from July to September 1837 it was again under Elizabeth Hamblin's management.

Elizabeth Hamblin had been a popular actress at Thomas Hamblin's Bowery Theatre until marital difficulties forced her from that stage. According to her friend Mary Clarke, Thomas Hamblin was an abusive husband, who had several mistresses. Elizabeth Hamblin's extensive work as an actress, despite bearing seven children (two survived infancy) in a dozen years, helped support the family, but exercising a husband's perogative, Thomas Hamblin regularly pocketed her income.[17] Hamblin further antagonized his wife by recruiting and training women of ill repute to appear on the Bowery stage. When the couple eventually divorced, Thomas Hamblin was forbidden to marry again during Elizabeth's lifetime, and she was awarded a $600-a-year settlement. In need of cash about a year later, Elizabeth Hamblin agreed to a one-time final settlement of $2,500. Joseph Ireland reported that she used this sum to launch her theatre management.[18]

In her management of the Richmond Hill Theatre, Elizabeth Hamblin made a deliberate attempt to distinguish her style from that of her former husband. She made no attempt to rival Thomas Hamblin in terms of scenic spectacle, a contest she had no hope of winning, instead concentrating on smaller scale entertainments. Elizabeth Hamblin also attempted to present slightly more refined plays, as suited her style of acting, rather than appeal to the lowest common denominator of popular taste. As a manager, she was able to create a stage where she could work, control her own income, and begin to establish her independent career.

Even though Elizabeth Hamblin's management never threatened to eclipse the fame of Thomas Hamblin, in the summer of 1837 her presence as a manager must have been almost intolerable for him. Following the destruction of the Bowery Theatre by fire in September 1836, the ground had been leased to William Dinneford, who rebuilt the theatre and became its manager. Hamblin did not resume management of the Bowery (rebuilt after yet another fire) until May 1839.[19] Temporarily without a theatre of his own, Thomas Hamblin was enraged when his former wife produced *Every One Has His Fault* in August 1837 with their young son William in the cast, and he attempted unsuccessfully to stop the performance and to gain custody of the child.[20]

Elizabeth Hamblin continued to accept acting engagements at various theatres and took a couple more turns at management. In May and June 1838 she managed a short season in the new Olympic Theatre at 444 Broadway.[21] After her marriage to James Charles, a member of her first Richmond Hill company, she managed a season of musical entertainments at the newly christened Tivoli Garden, formerly the Richmond Hill. This season, which ran from 29 June to 14 September 1840, undoubtedly shared some attractions with the Colonade Garden in Brooklyn Heights, a second theatre managed by Mrs. Charles from 3 August to 28 September 1840.[22] Elizabeth Hamblin Charles continued to appear as an actress, mostly in the Southwest, until her death on 8 May 1849.

ANNETTE NELSON

Interrupting Elizabeth Hamblin's 1836–37 tenure at the Richmond Hill, Annette Nelson managed the theatre from 12 October to 7 December 1836. An English actress who came to New Orleans in 1833 and had just made her first New York appearance on 24 September 1836, Nelson specialized in singing, dancing, and looking beautiful in spectacular pieces. Miss Nelson's Theatre featured many of the same actors who had performed for the previous management, and on a few occasions Elizabeth Hamblin herself appeared. Making her own best efforts in pieces like *The Deep, Deep Sea*, Nelson also produced plays such as *Othello*, *The Rent Day*, *George Barnwell*, and *The Victim of Treachery*, in which she relied on Virginia Monier to handle most of the heavy business. Nelson evidently believed that the more substantial fare was necessary to attract a regular audience, especially because a company in the small Richmond Hill Theatre could not compete on the basis of spectacle alone. Unfortunately, Nelson lacked the managerial advantage of being a strong actress herself. Not long after giving up management, Nelson married Copleston Coward Hodges and performed with him in the South. In 1847 she married theatre manager John Brougham and returned to the New York stage, though increasing obesity led her to premature retirement, years before her death in 1870. Brougham's first wife, Emma, later had a brief career as a manager, giving Brougham the distinction of having had two wives in the management business, though neither was married to him at the time of her managerial career.[23]

VIRGINIA MONIER

An actress in the Richmond Hill companies of both Hamblin and Nelson, Virginia Monier launched her own theatrical enterprise, Miss Monier's Dramatic Saloon, on 14 August 1837 in a small, recently converted space known as the City Theatre, in the upper level of a building called the City Saloon. Monier was the daughter of actors and had appeared on the New York stage as a child.[24] Besides presenting herself in popular melodramas such as *The Hunchback*, *The Stranger*, and *Zarah; or, The Gypsey's Revenge*, Monier featured her younger sister Eliza in children's roles including Little Pickle. The Dramatic Saloon was not a success. It closed in September 1837, but the young manager evidently attracted attention to her acting abilities, and the following May she assumed the role of leading lady at the National Theatre.[25]

Monier returned to management in 1840 with greater success, leasing a theatre in Washington, D.C., which apparently had not been popular with other managers. The *Spirit of the Times* reported:

Miss Monier has...taken the management of the Washington theatre. It has proved hitherto a burdensome and unprofitable responsibility, chiefly in consequence of the excessive number of free admissions. It seems cruel for a young and pretty woman, and withal a clever actress, to assume such annoying cares; but we are strongly in hopes that the gallantry of the inhabitants of the District will induce them to renounce their free admissions [and] to support liberally the new management.[26]

The locals supported Monier's management from October 1840 through February 1841. Then she assumed the management of the Avon Theatre, Norfolk, Virginia, from 20 March until 15 May 1841. Monier presumably returned to the Washington Theatre, where she was to receive a benefit sometime after 28 August 1841 when she relinquished her management of the establishment.[27]

Reflecting on the odds against these women managers in New York City, Odell notes that "one is amazed at the temerity of Mrs. Hamblin and Miss Monier in venturing to compete in their hot little theatres and with inferior actors, with such an array in the cool theatre of Niblo's Garden."[28] The competition at Niblo's Garden included an acting company with John Sefton, Joseph Jefferson, and Clara Fisher Maeder; vocalists, T. Bishop, Mrs. Knight, and Mrs. Bishop; and the Ravel troupe of acrobats. Yet, Elizabeth Hamblin and Virginia Monier were concerned not so much with surpassing all competition as with showcasing their own talents. Hamblin, Monier, Annette Nelson, and Charlotte Baldwin did not stay in management for long, and none of them was among the most successful or influential theatre managers in New York during the first half of the nineteenth century. For these women managing a theatre was a temporary measure, a demonstration of individual initiative when suitable employment in another theatre was unavailable.

At the very least, each of these women was able to gather a company, secure a theatre, and mount several productions. They selected their repertory from traditional fare and aimed to please popular taste. Certainly, these women did not present a challenge to society in their choice of plays. Their productions varied from those at the major houses primarily by being smaller in scale, employing fewer professional actors and, presumably, less scenery than the larger theatres. The small scale of operations was most likely determined by the women's inability to attract significant investment for their business enterprises at that time. The two more successful managers of this group, Hamblin and Monier, benefited from increased familiarity with the management business. Elizabeth Hamblin had been able to observe a theatre manager at work while married to Thomas Hamblin. Monier, not discouraged by the short duration of her New York management, apparently decided she would have greater success in an area with less competing theatrical activity. Her management of theatres in Washington, D.C., and Virginia was for a longer period than her initial foray into management and indicates that she had learned something from her New York experience. Remarkably, the managerial activities of all four women seem to have been carried out with little fuss about women's proper sphere. All four were professional performers who entered management when it seemed to be a good career move.

FRANCES ANNE DENNY DRAKE

Another woman manager and a true pioneer was Frances Anne Denny Drake. Born on 6 November 1797 in Schenectady, New York, she was living with her widowed mother, an innkeeper in Albany, when Samuel Drake and family arrived in town in 1813 and made preparations for their western journey. Added to the ranks of the Drake troupe before their departure for Kentucky in the spring of 1814, the inexperienced Denny learned a great deal performing with the company at each stop along the route, and was soon showing signs of the acting talent that would win her the appellation "star of the west."[29] Around 1818 Denny moved back east and performed in the more competitive arena of the larger cities, making her New York debut as Helen Worrett at the Park Theatre on 17 April 1820, but the next year she rejoined the Drakes in Cincinnati. She married Samuel Drake's son Alexander early in 1822, and assisted him in the management of the Louisville Theatre and the Cincinnati Theatre from 1824 until his death in 1830, a period during which she had four children and also played short engagements in other cities.

Frances Drake's acting abilities were praised in Mrs. Trollope's *Domestic Manners of the Americans*, though Trollope, typically critical of things American, observed that the Cincinnati Theatre's patrons were ill mannered and not numerous enough to provide sufficient revenue for decorating and cleaning the small house.[30]   Drake continued her acting career after her husband's death, and in 1839 she came to the assistance of Samuel Drake, then past seventy, by assuming the management of the Louisville City Theatre, which he owned.   Managing the theatre from January 1839 to January 1840, Frances Drake presented plays such as *The Devil and Dr. Faustus*, *The Maid of Orleans*, and *La Tour de Nesle*, and also novelty acts.   She depended on short appearances by traveling actors and during the summer season had the good fortune to attract Edwin Forrest, Junius Brutus Booth, and Dan Marble to her theatre.   Leaving the stage and management to marry George Washington Cutter, a marriage which lasted only a few months, she performed only on rare occasions in her later years until her death on 11 February 1874.[31]

MARY ELIZABETH MAYWOOD

Two more women theatre managers appeared in Philadelphia in 1842, both of them young and one destined for great fame as an actress.   Just twenty years old when she was named manager of the Chestnut Street Theatre, Mary Elizabeth Maywood had slight acting experience including appearances as Bianca in *Fazio* at the Haymarket in London and at the Park Theatre, New York, where she was not a critical success.   Her appointment as manager was due to the recommendation of her father, Robert Maywood, who had managed the Chestnut Street Theatre from 1831 until 1839, when the stockholders offered the lease to Lewis Pratt.   After Pratt ran into financial difficulties, the stockholders invited Maywood back, but he proposed instead that his daughter take the job, with himself as business manager and Peter Richings as stage manager.   Thus assisted, Mary Elizabeth Maywood on 17 September 1842 began what Francis Courtney Wemyss called her "petticoat government," a term frequently used to describe and belittle women's managerial efforts.[32] Maywood herself did not make any premature claims concerning her managerial abilities, and her playbill stated:

> Miss Mary Elizabeth Maywood respectfully informs the Public that she has leased the CHESTNUT STREET THEATRE for the present season, and with great diffidence relies on the generous and enlightened support which has ever characterized the taste of PHILADELPHIA. MISS MAYWOOD believes that it would be vain to make large promises at the commencement, but she presumes to say that every exertion shall be used to render this favorite establishment a scene of attraction.[33]

Maywood had reason to be thankful she had not made any large promises, for despite her exertions her management was not prosperous. Assisted by visiting stars, Madame Celeste, Mr. and Mrs. John Brougham, and Junius Brutus Booth, and by Dr. Lardner whose lectures on the French Revolution were illustrated by actors in historical tableaux, Maywood kept her company busy with frequent changes of bill. Then on 5 December 1842 she changed tactics and presented a season of opera lasting through 17 February 1843. Wemyss reported:

> The receipts of the opera season, which must have paid the stars, does not appear to have satisfied the fair manageress, whose unpaid bills and actors' salaries became, thus early, a source of annoyance. She published a foolish card in the newspapers, stating the sum received by the opera troupe, and the amount lost by the theatre. If the object was to excite sympathy or commiseration, it failed to produce either.[34]

As performers did not generally settle for less than the terms of their engagement just because a manager was facing hard times, the public was probably amused at the naïveté revealed in Maywood's grievance. In a final effort to have a profitable season Maywood turned to concerts beginning 13 May 1843, but this too proved unsuccessful, with the number of musicians diminishing each week. On 31 July 1843 she resigned her management of the theatre.[35]

CHARLOTTE CUSHMAN

Soon after Mary Elizabeth Maywood was selected as the new manager of the Chestnut Street, Ethelbert A. Marshall, lessee of the Walnut Street Theatre, invited Charlotte Cushman to assume management of his theatre, presumably hoping to profit by creating a public rivalry between the two women, and depriving the Chestnut Street of the novelty of having the only ''lady manager'' in town. Marshall may have heard the idea then being circulated in New York that Cushman showed great artistic promise and should be given her own theatre.[36] Twenty-six-year-old Cushman outlasted her managerial competition, but she had a difficult time because several of the company members apparently did not like to take instructions from a woman, especially one who was young and relatively inexperienced. Though beginning to show much promise, Cushman was not yet recognized as the great actress she would become, and she struggled to study new roles and perfect her acting while taking on the extra burden of management.

Cushman presented a season of varied offerings with the aid of several visiting performers including John Sefton, George Vandenhoff, Edwin Forrest, Henry Placide, Mr. and Mrs. John Brougham, Junius Brutus Booth, William

Burton, and Yankee actors James Hackett, George Handel Hill, Dan Marble, and Josh Silsbee, some of whom may have been engaged before Cushman assumed management of the theatre. This was a good array of stars, but not exceptional, as it was fairly easy to attract stars to a major theatrical city such as Philadelphia. Marshall had hoped that the novelty of a female management would draw an audience, but Cushman's presence did not seem to add to the receipts. Besides the fact that the company was not clearly gaining anything from Cushman's management, the rather artificial circumstances by which she was promoted to management made it difficult for her to control the company. Cushman did not have the same authority of a West or Merry, who had held leading positions as actresses within their companies for years, in addition to their close association with the previous managers from whom they inherited the right to manage. Cushman also lacked the authority of the women who had demonstrated initiative by starting their own small theatres from scratch and hiring their own companies. At the end of the first season William Rufus Blake took over as manager in effect, though he was announced as Cushman's assistant in order to save her from public embarrassment. Still, Cushman, who had been the frequent target of Blake's jokes in front of the rest of the company, must have found her removal from power rather humiliating.[37]

In the fall of 1843 Cushman played opposite William Charles Macready when he visited Philadelphia, and at his suggestion she went to England the next year and soon established herself as a star. Though Wemyss predicted that Cushman could someday be a great theatre lessee and manager in New York City, her experience at the Walnut was discouraging and she never again attempted management. According to Wemyss, both Cushman and Maywood "discovered that they were out of their proper sphere of action; that the energy of a Madame Vestris, the only female who ever successfully conducted a theatre, did not belong to either of them."[38] Yet, these two women did demonstrate a good deal of energy, presenting several changes of bill each week. It seems more likely that they lacked sufficient theatrical experience and maturity, rather than energy. While neither drew big enough houses to make a profit after paying for stars, their contemporaries did not criticize their managements as artistic failures. In his discussion of the managements of Maywood and Cushman (part of a history of Philadelphia theatre, published during the 1850s), Charles Durang wrote:

> We have now to record a new era in theatrical Institutions, the establishment of a precedent whereby females might reign supreme on the theatric throne as well as the lordly sex. We do not know a profession or business where females have more autocratic sway and influential power than in the cabinet councils of theatrical management. They stand before the public as the enchanting representatives of the softer sex, whose influences rule half the world. Their incomes in the dramatic vocation average those of the best male

actors. No important drama can be produced without their aid....Nor do we know one other profession that so eminently assigns to women such high duties.[39]

Durang recognized that a number of women were finding unusual professional opportunities in the theatre. Though neither Maywood nor Cushman personally prospered as managers, they helped open the way for other women, as Philadelphia audiences became acquainted with the possibility of women theatre managers.

ANNE SEFTON

While preparing to relieve Charlotte Cushman of managerial responsibilities in the spring of 1843, William R. Blake must have been somewhat surprised to learn that his stepdaughter, Anne Duff Waring Sefton, had assumed the management of a theatre in New Orleans. Anne's father, Leigh Waring, had died soon after she was born in 1815, and her mother, Caroline Placide, later married Blake. Making her debut on 27 September 1828 for the Blakes' benefit at the Chatham Theatre, New York, Anne Waring appeared at various New York theatres during the next few years, including the Bowery and the National. She married actor William Sefton in 1837 and was widowed in 1839. Moving to New Orleans, where she had many family ties, Anne Sefton acted for James Caldwell in December 1842 at his newly rebuilt American Theatre. After Caldwell resigned from its management and William Dinneford had taken a brief managerial stint, on 21 February 1843 Mrs. Sefton became the manager of the American.

In a contemporary report Joe Cowell observed, "Mrs. Sefton now had the control: the company was small, but her superior talent and experienced energy made it respectably effective."[40] Her first season featured visiting actors George Vandenhoff, J. H. Kirby, Augustus Addams, and George Holland, as well as a troupe of Swiss pantomimists, and it ended with a benefit for the actress-manager on 14 May 1843. She earned a benefit exerting herself not only as a manager but as an actress. The reviewer for the *Picayune* observed:

> Mrs. Sefton, if much labor and close attention to business is entitled to success, certainly deserves to be rewarded. She not only manages the New American, but we see her on the same evening playing *Lady MacBeth* and one of the broom girls in "Buy it, Dear." Then again as the musing and dreaming *Ion*, and on the same night personating perhaps *Don Juan*, or some other equally light character—and in all she appears equally at home.[41]

Before the next season, which began on 11 November 1843, Sefton ran large ads in the New York–based *Spirit of the Times*, announcing the renovation of the interior of the American Theatre and recruiting new company members and visiting stars.[42] She engaged as leading man and stage manager James W. Wallack, Jr., whom she had apparently already married though she continued to use the name Sefton while in New Orleans. Despite appearances by William Burton, John Brougham, George Handel Hill, Dan Marble, Mrs. Sequin's English Opera Company, and others, Sefton failed to attract enough business. Residents of New Orleans could chose from a wide variety of entertainments including ballroom dancing, French language theatre at the Orleans Theatre, and equestrian drama at the National Amphitheatre, but the most damaging competition facing Sefton was the New St. Charles Theatre, under the management of Noah Ludlow and Sol Smith. The enterprising Ludlow and Smith controlled a large circuit of theatres and were, thus, in a position to secure the most popular touring stars for the St. Charles. On 29 February 1844, at a performance of *The Honeymoon*, Sefton made a curtain speech asking for public support, but she was able to continue the season for only another month, officially ending her management on 13 April 1844 and taking a benefit on 29 March.[43] In later years she was known as Mrs. Wallack and frequently performed in New York and in England before her death on 11 February 1879.[44]

ELIZABETH JEFFERSON RICHARDSON

During Anne Sefton's management of the American Theatre, Elizabeth Jefferson Richardson managed a theatre for a short time in another Southern city, Mobile, Alabama. Born in 1810, the daughter of Joseph Jefferson, Sr., Elizabeth made a rather inauspicious stage debut at the Chestnut Street Theatre, Philadelphia, in 1827 and soon married the actor Samuel Chapman, who died within a year. The young widow's acting was much improved by the 1834–35 season, when she appeared at the Park Theatre in New York and was perceived as a good all-around actress with musical ability. Mrs. Chapman retired from the stage in 1835 upon her marriage to a printer, Augustus Richardson, but she returned to the Park the next year, after her second husband also met a premature death.

For the 1841–42 season Elizabeth Richardson found a job acting in the company at the Mobile Theatre (also known as the Royal Street Theatre). The following season she secured employment in the company for her brother, Joseph Jefferson II, who died in November; his two children; her sisters and their husbands, Mr. MacKenzie and Mr. Wright; and her niece Effie Germon and her husband. The theatre, owned by James Caldwell, had been leased to local businessmen E. DeVandel and Jules Dumas, and was managed by Charles Fisher and stage-managed by Coppleston Hodges, husband of former New York theatre manager Annette Nelson. Unfortunately, the season managed by

Fisher ended in March, leaving the Jefferson clan stranded in Mobile without other likely job prospects. In order to keep her family members employed, Elizabeth Richardson elected to manage the theatre for a summer season beginning in April 1843. A member of the company who left one week into the summer season after receiving his benefit, Joe Cowell reported:

> All the engagements terminated at the end of twenty weeks, which closed the season; but a few members of the company with small salaries, who could afford to accept one third, or even half of their former income, or, to speak plainly, who could not afford to go without any income at all, commenced a new campaign under the management of Mrs. Richardson, instead of Mr. Hodges. Madame Vestris, I believe, was the first to set this fashion of petticoat government, which has been followed, with various claims to popularity in this country, by Miss Cushman, Miss Maywood, Miss Virginia Monier, Miss Clarendon, Mrs. Sefton, and now Mrs. Richardson, I am grieved to say, lent her name to eke out the very small demands on public favour of only half a company, half paid.[45]

Hodges, the logical managerial candidate in Cowell's opinion, did continue to act with the company, but must not have wanted to assume the risk or lend his name to the summer management. Cowell's comment indicates that a tendency toward women in management was already observable by 1844, at least to a man of the theatre. After the summer in Mobile, the Jeffersons followed their separate career paths. Elizabeth Richardson married Charles Fisher in 1849, and after his death in 1854 she taught music during some of her later years before her own death on 18 November 1890.[46]

MATILDA CLARENDON

Joe Cowell also reported that a local newspaper had announced that the new American Theatre in Mobile would be under the management of a woman, one described by Cowell as young and pretty and the originator of the role of Grace Harkaway at the Park—which could only be Matilda Clarendon.[47] Despite the announcement in the Mobile *Register and Journal* that she would assume management of the new establishment on 26 April 1843, Clarendon's ambition was checked by "circumstances beyond her control."[48] She did, however, soon find work as the manager of the Pittsburgh Theatre.

A young woman more noted for beauty than acting ability, Matilda Clarendon had first appeared at the Park Theatre, New York, in April 1841, and on 11 October 1841 she played Grace Harkaway in the American premiere of Boucicault's *London Assurance*, only to be replaced a few days later. Clarendon had been cast in the role due to the influence of Park Benjamin, editor of the *New World* and Clarendon's benefactor, and her failure in the role invited sharp criticism from other papers.[49] Undaunted, Clarendon took to the road and by the beginning of 1842 was starring with the G. Hoffman Company, when it traveled through Utica, New York. At the end of that engagement in early March she presented a program of dramatic readings in Utica, billing herself as from the Park Theatre. Besides delivering a number of monologues and scenes, mainly Shakespearean, the resourceful Clarendon made the best of her New York experience by presenting imitations of the main characters in *London Assurance* as acted at the Park.[50] When Clarendon played a star engagement at Caldwell's American Theatre in New Orleans during January 1843, tackling such plays as *Venice Preserved*, *King Lear*, and *The School for Scandal*, the local press criticized her acting though not her "youthful loveliness."[51] As leading lady at the American under Dinneford's short management, Clarendon once again pulled out her imitations of Charlotte Cushman, Henry Placide, William Wheatley, and herself in *London Assurance*. Acting for two weeks under Anne Sefton's management of the American, she resigned after playing Julia in Knowles's *The Hunchback* on 8 March 1843.

Beginning on 30 August 1843 Clarendon performed a star engagement at the Pittsburgh Theatre, which was under the management of William P. Hastings. It is not clear how long Clarendon intended to play at the theatre, but on 5 September Hastings and his company were temporarily dislodged from the theatre. They were replaced by the lecturer Dr. Lardner, who presumably paid theatre owner Simpson a hefty sum to accommodate him. The Pittsburgh Theatre briefly reopened under Hastings's management on 20 September, but within a week a local paper reported that the theatre would soon be under the management of Clarendon.[52] Other possible managers were also rumored to have plans for the theatre, with the result that for most of the winter it remained empty. By the beginning of March 1844 Clarendon was again a prime candidate, and the *Spirit of the Times* announced that the Pittsburgh Theatre would open immediately under her sole management.[53] The opening eventually occurred on 10 April 1844.

Clarendon's management did not begin smoothly. She had traveled south to recruit actors, but many of the performers she engaged did not arrive for the first week of her season. On 15 April the *Chronicle* reported:

> The Manageress, we hear, has thus far, had many difficulties to surmount, principally growing out of the nonarrival, in season of several of the Stock Actors, with whom positive engagements have been made, but we are assured that the stock will be full in a day or two. The judicious management of a Theatre, with its cares, troubles and anxieties, is truly a herculean task, and the lady manageress has thus far evinced an energy of character and power of discrimination beyond her years, which would do honor to a veteran manager, and

richly entitle her to the admiration and support of the friends of the theatre.[54]

Clarendon told the audience that although she had even paid transportation costs for some of the actors, managers in Cincinnati and Lexington were attempting to prevent the actors from traveling to Pittsburgh. By 19 April, Clarendon had resorted to presenting a variety program instead of plays, and on 22 April she decided to close the theatre for a few nights until more actors could be found.[55] Her difficulty in recruiting seems to have been primarily due to timing—it was late in the season, but still too early for most actors to be looking for summer work. The fact that she was a woman and unknown as a manager probably made it difficult for some actors to trust her guarantee of a salary.

Clarendon was able to reopen the theatre on 25 April, and her season ran through 17 June 1844. The *Post* reported, "She has been subjected to unusual vexation during the season, and has realized nothing from the management, but has, nevertheless, had the gratification of overcoming the most formidable obstacles to the future success of the Drama in Pittsburgh."[56] Evidently, Clarendon did find some gratification in managing the Pittsburgh Theatre because she chose to manage another season. Her actors, perhaps not receiving their full salaries, did not share her enthusiasm, and in the fall she was supported by an entirely new company.

Clarendon's second season began on 4 September and came to an early end on 23 October 1844. Clarendon attracted national attention, but also precipitated the end of her management when she horsewhipped Mr. Simpson, proprietor of the theatre. The exact details of this incident remain unclear. Though there was some speculation that this was a publicity stunt, Clarendon claimed that, friendless and unprotected, she was merely seeking retaliation for an insult she had received the previous season, and that as she had not told anyone of her intentions, she clearly was not seeking publicity.[57] After ending her management, Clarendon made another Pittsburgh appearance, presenting a program of dramatic readings at Duquesne Hall. According to the *Post* she gave "a brief statement of the occurrences which took place on the closing of the Theatre, and the course of the strange events of that evening."[58] Unfortunately, a fuller explanation of the exact nature of Clarendon's dispute with Simpson was not provided. Despite conflicts with the theatre owner and fierce competition with managers in other cities for actors, Clarendon was fairly successful as a manager. She presented two short seasons of plays in a city that had previously witnessed only a few seasons of professional theatre.

MADAME DE MARGUERITTES

Like Matilda Clarendon, the colorful Madame de Marguerittes also made news by physically confronting her opposition. Born in France, Julia Granville was married to the Count de Marguerittes and moved to the United States. When the count abandoned her and returned to France, she supported herself by giving readings and concerts. She later married George "Gaslight" Foster, author of such books as *New York Naked* and *New York by Gaslight*, but she kept the dramatic name Madame de Marguerittes. Moving from concerts into opera, Madame de Marguerittes made a few New York City appearances—for example, in *La Gazza Ladra* on 9 March 1852 at the Broadway and in *Maid of Paillisseau* on 16 March 1852 at the Lyceum—before embarking on a starring tour. Arriving in Albany and finding the Green Street Theatre vacant, she decided to take up management.

Built in 1812, the Green Street had been used as a church from 1819 until 1852, when it was reconverted into a theatre and opened on 5 July 1852 under the management of Henry W. (or William S.) Preston, who had previously managed Albany's Pearl Street Theatre. Albany historian Joel Munsell reported, "On the 12th August following the performances were brought to a close by the sheriff, who took out the scenery," and Preston soon lost his control of the theatre.[59] Before reopening the Green Street, Madame de Marguerittes conducted a thorough renovation and redecoration, completed with the novelty of a mirrored front curtain which cost $1,500. A correspondent for the *Spirit of the Times* reported that the fashionable crowd was stopping by to see the elegant theatre, especially the drop curtain of mirrors, and observed:

> The manager, who is no more afraid of a Latin *jeu de mot* than she is afraid of paint and scaffolding, threatens to have "Veluti in Speculum" inscribed above it. She it is who has given the design for this drop, as well as for the whole decorations. As we all know, from her writings, she is a woman of imagination; but, thank the Gods! she is a practical woman; and so, there she is, all day, in a dark shaggy cloak, and an unpretending bonnet, pencil and book in hand, drawing, talking, and explaining, from the furnaces under the stage to the highest scaffolding.[60]

Though this particular account may have been written by Madame de Marguerittes or her husband, "Gaslight" Foster, there is no doubt that she energetically redecorated before beginning her season.[61] Finally, on 20 December 1852, Madame de Marguerittes opened the Green Street with *Don Caesar de Bazan* and *The Irish Valet*, presented by a company that included the not-yet-famous Joseph Jefferson III.

The company seemed to be off to a good start, but former manager Preston, who had not been happy to lose his theatre, resented the attention the theatre was receiving, especially because the new manager was a woman. On 12 January 1852 Preston created an exciting scene when he decided to seize control of the theatre, and the *Spirit of the Times* reported:

> Mr. Preston, the former manager, having been fouled to get possession of the premises by legal means, resorted to violent measures, and entered with a gang of his associates, about 7 o'clock in the morning. Madame de Marguerittes being apprised of the event, hastened to the spot, and, at the head of the police force, battered down the stage door and took possession. She was the first to enter the building, and, rushing on the stage, found that the whole gang, with Preston at their head, had made their escape through a back door into an alley, and so to the street.[62]

A few blows were exchanged in the street, and even Madame de Marguerittes was struck on the hand, but she had defended her occupation of the theatre and gained new public support, as the citizens of Albany expressed their indignation at Preston's behavior. "The greatest feeling [was] expressed in favor of Madame de Marguerittes, as well as admiration for her courageous maintenance of her rights. She is quite the lion of the day."[63] Madame de Marguerittes continued with her season, presenting *London Assurance* and Alfred B. Street's adaptation of *Uncle Tom's Cabin* with herself, short, stout, and gray-haired, as Eva, but in February her management ended. Henry Phelps recalled:

> We are safe in saying that no woman ever came into Albany who created more of a sensation in so short a time, than the Madame. Her plans were all on a grand scale. She had two houses on Hamilton street, for dressing rooms to the theatre, and a mansion on Madison avenue, for a residence. She had a room in the theatre, devoted to the use of newspaper men, and in short, displayed enterprise far beyond anything seen here before. It was a pity she did not have a fairer chance.[64]

The cost of her extravagant managerial style, combined with pressure from the remaining Preston faction, was enough to persuade Madame de Marguerittes to abandon the project. In later years she worked as a music critic and wrote several plays and dramatizations from novels including *Darrel Markham; or, The Captain of the Vulture*, *Rosel; or, The Christmas Tree*, *Aurora Floyd*, and *Enoch Arden*, a piece played with great success by Edwin Adams.[65]

MARIE DURET

Another New York town, Utica, hosted a woman theatre manager, Marie Duret, the next year. Duret, who had already achieved some popularity performing in the Southwest, appeared at several New York City theatres in the spring of 1850. By 1853 she had organized her own company and established herself as the manager of the Museum in Utica. Her season, which began on 5 September, featured several visiting star performers and tended toward the spectacular and melodramatic. It included *Alladin; or, The Wonderful Lamp*, *Flowers of the Forest*, *Zarah; or, The Gypsey's Revenge*, and *Jack Sheppard; or, The Housebreaker of the Last Century*. The last play provided Duret with a lively breeches role that called for scaling walls and being hung at the gallows, and she kept it in her repertory for years. Also included in the Utica season was a local interest piece called *The Utica Fireman*.[66] On 11 January 1854, after five months as a manager, Duret was quietly and quickly replaced by Mr. Roth, the theatre's owner, though she continued to perform at the Museum for the rest of the season.[67] Marie Duret eventually returned to the Southwest where she traveled supported by her own company for many years, and later she gave lessons in dramatic elocution but was reduced to poverty, and died in San Francisco in April 1881.[68]

At least fifteen women, as shown in this chapter, had been theatre managers or proprietors by 1853, before Keene or Sinclair entered the arena. Keene's career, though an unprecedented success for a woman in this country, was not a complete aberration, and some theatre workers, at least, must have been aware of a woman or two who had managed a theatre. In general these women had respectable though short terms of management. Most took up management out of necessity, filling the role of a manager who died or organizing a small new company to support their own starring efforts, but a few of these managers also demonstrated personal ambition in launching their ventures. Some of the greatest American actresses, most notably Merry and Cushman, were managers for a time, as were women who clearly displayed more ingenuity and initiative than acting talent. One bold woman manager, Madame de Marguerittes, even came to the physical defense of her theatre when such action proved necessary.

Working in several different cities, these women responded to various individual circumstances which put them in a position to try managing a theatre. All were unusual for their day in supporting themselves by working outside their homes, holding leadership positions, supervising male employees, and concerning themselves with the practical and business aspects of the theatre. There is no evidence that their activities were viewed with alarm or seen as a challenge to the social order. Perhaps this is because their theatrical enterprises tended to be on a small scale, lasting only a season or two. Also, these women did not disturb the status quo through the type of entertainment they provided. They presented the same plays or types of plays and, when they engaged stars, the same stars that could be seen in theatres run by men. Further, in most cases the activities of a woman theatre manager appeared to be an isolated occurrence. Although several women ventured into management in the first half of the nineteenth century, their efforts did not constitute a recognizable movement. During the 1850s the unique historical situation of the Gold Rush encouraged several women to attempt theatre management in California, and their efforts will be discussed in the next chapter.

NOTES

1. Susanne K. Sherman, "Thomas Wade West, Theatrical Impressario, 1790–1799," *William and Mary Quarterly,* 3d ser., 9 (January 1952): 18.

2. Susanne K. Sherman, "Post-Revolutionary Theatre in Virginia" (Master's thesis, College of William and Mary, 1950), 218–20.

3. Ibid., 228.

4. Additional information on Margaretta Sully West from Martin Staples Shockley, *The Richmond Stage 1784–1812* (Charlottesville: University Press of Virginia, 1977), and [Thomas Wade] West Company entry by Weldon B. Durham and Jerri Cummins Crawford in Durham, ed., *American Theatre Companies, 1749–1887* (New York: Greenwood Press, 1986), 548–53.

5. Gresdna Ann Doty, *The Career of Mrs. Anne Brunton Merry in the American Theatre* (Baton Rouge: Louisiana State University Press, 1971), 108.

6. Charles Durang, "The Philadelphia Stage, from the Year 1749 to the Year 1855. Partly Compiled from the Papers of His Father, the Late John Durang, with Notes by the Editors [of the Philadelphia *Sunday Dispatch*]" 7 May 1854 to 8 July 1860. Microfilm copy, New York Public Library at Lincoln Center, of scrapbooks in the University of Pennsylvania library, 78.

7. Doty, 119, 126.

8. George O. Willard, *History of the Providence Stage 1762–1891* (Providence: Rhode Island News Company, 1891). Willard does not make absolutely clear that the manager of the Providence theatre was Snelling rather than Charles Powell and does not state that Mrs. Powell became lessee because her husband had died, although this can be inferred.

9. Francis Courtney Wemyss, *Wemyss' Chronology of the American Stage from 1752 to 1852* (New York: William Taylor and Company, 1852), 184. Date of management not given. Also, Willard reports that Mrs. Powell's daughter Elizabeth married Henry J. Finn (p. 88).

10. Ruth Crosby Dimmick, *Our Theatre To-day and Yesterday* (New York: H. K. Fly Company, 1913), 25.

11. George C. D. Odell, *Annals of the New York Stage* (New York: Columbia University Press, 1927–41; New York: AMS Press, 1970), 2:198, 216.

12. Ibid., 3:33.

13. Joseph N. Ireland, *Records of the New York Stage from 1750 to 1860* (New York, 1866–67; New York: Burt Franklin, 1968), 1:416.

14. Ireland reported that Mrs. Hamblin received a $3,000 divorce settlement which she used to begin her managerial career; ibid., 462.

15. Odell, 4:102–3.

16. Ibib., 169.

17. M[ary] Clarke, A Concise History of the Life and Amours of Thomas S. Hamblin, Late Manager of the Bowery Theatre, As Communicated by His Legal Wife, Mrs. Elizabeth Hamblin, to Mrs. M. Clarke. (Philadelphia and New York, n.d.). Although the title seems to suggest that the work was published after Thomas Hamblin's death in 1853, a close reading indicates that it was written earlier. Quite possibly "Late Manager" simply indicates that Hamblin was no longer manager of the Bowery, as was the case in the late 1830s. The author claims to be writing in response to a pro-Hamblin piece, which appeared in the June 1837 *Lady's Companion*. It seems likely that this pamphlet appeared between 1837 and 1839. Copy in Boston Public Library, Rare Books and Manuscripts Collection.

18. Ireland, 1:462.

19. Rosemarie K. Bank, "Bowery Theatre Company," in Durham, 116.

20. Ireland, 2:210.

21. Odell, 4:252–53.

22. Ibid., 434–36. Ireland noted that Mrs. Hamblin also managed a theatre in Petersburg, Virginia (p. 462).

23. Information on Annette Nelson from Odell 4:170–71, Ireland 2:178–79, 210, and T. Allston Brown, *A History of the New York Stage* (New York: Dodd, Mead, and Company, 1903), 1:235.

24. Wemyss, *Wemyss' Chronology*, 102. In this not especially reliable book, Wemyss reports that Mrs. Monier managed a theatre on the island of Jamaica. Other sources place Virginia's mother in Jamaica but do not confirm that she was a manager.

25. Odell, 4:174–75, Ireland, 2:82–83, 211, Dimmick, 30.

26. *Spirit of the Times*, 17 October 1840, 396.

27. Ibid., 28 August 1841, 312.

28. Odell, 4:180–82.

29. George D. Ford, *These Were Actors: A Story of the Chapmans and the Drakes* (New York: Library Publishers, 1955), 173.

30. Mrs. [Frances] Trollope, *Domestic Manners of the Americans* (London: Whittaker, Treacher and Company, 1832), 1:183–85.

31. James Walton Swain, "Mrs. Alexander Drake: A Biographical Study" (Ph.D. diss., Tulane University, 1970).

32. Francis Courtney Wemyss, *Twenty-Six Years in the Life of an Actor and Manager* (New York: Burgess, Stringer and Company, 1847), 378.

33. Playbill, Chestnut Street Theatre, 20 September 1842. In the Theatre

Collection of the Free Library of Philadelphia.

34. Wemyss, *Twenty-Six Years*, 380.

35. Arthur Herman Wilson, *A History of the Philadelphia Stage, 1835–1855* (Philadelphia: University of Pennsylvania Press, 1935; New York: Greenwood Press, 1968), and Durang, 205–8.

36. Joseph Leach, *Bright Particular Star: The Life and Times of Charlotte Cushman* (New Haven: Yale University Press, 1970), 106.

37. Wilson, 21, and Durang, 208–15.

38. Wemyss, *Twenty-Six Years*, 381.

39. Durang, 205.

40. Joe Cowell, *Thirty Years Passed among the Players in England and America* (New York: Harper and Brothers, 1844), 103.

41. *Picayune* (New Orleans), 22 March 1843, 2.

42. *Spirit of the Times*, 30 September 1843, 372. Also appeared 7, 14, and 21 October 1843.

43. Ibid., 9 March 1844, 24.

44. John S. Kendall, *The Golden Age of the New Orleans Theater* (Baton Rouge: Louisiana State University Press, 1952), 211, 232–34.

45. Cowell, 101.

46. William Winter, *Life and Art of Joseph Jefferson* (New York: Macmillan and Company, 1894), 127.

47. Cowell, 103.

48. Mobile *Register and Journal* 25 April and 3 May 1843, quoted in Mary Morgan Duggar, "The Theatre in Mobile 1822—1860" (Master's thesis, University of Alabama, 1941), 127–28.

49. Leach, 103–5.

50. Jack Hrkach, "Theatrical Activity and Other Popular Entertainment along the Turnpikes of New York State from the End of the American Revolution to the Beginnings of the Civil War" (Ph.D. diss., City University of New York, 1990), 166.

51. Kendall, 212.

52. *Aurora*, 26 September 1843, reported in Edward Garland Fletcher, "Records and History of Theatrical Activities in Pittsburgh, Pennsylvania, from Their Beginnings to 1861" (Ph.D. diss., Harvard University, 1931), 98.

53. *Spirit of the Times*, 2 March 1844, 12.

54. *Chronicle*, 15 April 1844, quoted in Fletcher, 102–3.

55. Fletcher, 104.

56. *Post* 17 June 1844, quoted in Fletcher, 105.

57. *Spirit of the Times*, 9 November 1844, 444; 16 November 1844, 456; 7 December 1844, 492.

58. *Post*, 2 November 1844, quoted in Fletcher, 109.

59. Joel Munsell, *Collections on the History of Albany* (Albany, N.Y.: J. Munsell, 1867), 2:34.

60. *Spirit of the Times*, 11 December 1852, 505.

61. H. P. Phelps, *A Record of the Albany Stage* (Albany, N.Y.: Joseph McDonough, 1880), 283.

62. *Spirit of the Times*, 22 January 1853, 583.

63. Ibid.

64. Phelps, 285.

65. Mention of Marguerittes's writing can be found in George Rogers Taylor, "Gaslight Foster: A New York 'Journeyman Journalist' at Mid-Century," *New York History* 58 (July 1977): 297–312, and in the *Spirit of the Times*, 11 June and 12 November 1864, 7 January 1865, 31 July 1869, and 25 May 1872.

66. Plays about firefighters were especially popular in this period. A favorite character, Mose, the fire "b'hoy", was first acted by Frank Chanfrau on 2 February 1848 in Ben Baker's *A Glance at New York* at the Olympic Theatre, New York. (B'hoy was a variation on boy, taken from a New York working-class social type, the Bowery B'hoy.) *The Utica Fireman* would appear to be a local variation on a theme. See Walter J. Meserve, *Heralds of Promise: The Drama of the American People during the Age of Jackson, 1829–1849* (New York: Greenwood Press, 1986), 120–27.

67. Hrkach, 256.

68. *New York Dramatic Mirror*, 23 April 1881, 7.

2

Women Theatre Managers of the California Gold Rush

The unique conditions of the California Gold Rush created previously unenvisioned opportunities for women to manage theatres in the 1850s in California. During the Gold Rush an enormous population increase in areas where professional theatres had not yet been established seemed to spark the imagination of enterprising would-be managers. The crowds, hungry for entertainment, supported even the crudest early attempts at theatrical presentations. Theatre was an enjoyable community activity, providing a break in the tedious routine of hard work or a diversion from boredom while waiting for snow to melt and mountain roads to become passable. Many new settlers may have found that the early California theatre, a reminder of the theatre they had attended in the East, eased their homesickness. Theatre managers also benefited. As Californians felt their wealth, both actual and potential, they spent freely, with a pinch of gold dust often serving as admission to a theatre.

The promising outlook for new theatrical ventures in California was especially encouraging for women. Miners welcomed any new theatre, whether run by a man or a woman. Certainly, a freer atmosphere existed in the less-than-stable new communities of California compared to the eastern United States, where community standards of respectability might check a woman's ambition to embark on a business enterprise, such as theatre management. Another factor favoring women was that with relatively few living in the territory, men were eager to see them onstage and to support their managerial efforts. Although prostitutes were the first women to provide a form of entertainment and to make a profit from the Gold Rush, many men also were happy to see "respectable women."[1] In the rough and wild California settlements, unlike the civilized East, actresses and women managers could easily assert their membership in the ranks of respectable womanhood. Women theatre managers were also perceived as having the potential to satisfy a desire for an entertainment more refined than drinking and gambling, one that might be suitable for women and children. As both performers and managers, women were welcomed enthusiastically as they appeared throughout the mining region from the major port of San Francisco to the inland cities of Sacramento, Stockton, and Marysville to the remotest mining camps.[2]

The promising conditions resulted in a greater concentration of women theatre managers than in any previous period in American history. Like their male counterparts, these women were eager to expand their prospects in the new California market, and they revealed more ambition than did earlier women managers in the United States. Consequently, their activities spread an awareness of the existence of women managers to a wider public.

SARAH KIRBY STARK

The first woman theatre manager in California, Sarah Kirby, arrived ahead of the hordes of eastern actors who hoped to mine gold as entertainers. Born in 1813, Sarah began her career as an actress on the East Coast and was married to J. Hudson Kirby, a popular young actor in heroic melodramas. After he died, while the pair were acting in England in 1848, Sarah returned to New York and married J. B. Wingerd (alternately, Wingered, Wingard, or Wingate). Traveling with Wingerd, Sarah arrived in California in January 1850 and made her first appearance as Pauline in Bulwer-Lytton's *The Lady of Lyons* on 21 February at Rowe's Amphitheatre in San Francisco. Joseph Rowe, the proprietor, had decided to present legitimate drama in addition to his equestrian and circus acts. This arrangement was not completely satisfactory to Sarah Kirby, who soon made plans with company member J. B. Atwater to open a theatre in Sacramento. Atwater had played in California's first professional theatre, the Eagle, Sacramento, from its opening on 18 October 1849, and served as manager from 13 November 1849 until flooded out on Christmas Eve. The flood-damaged Eagle Theatre was then purchased by Mr. McDowell, Mr. Fowler, and Mr. Warbass, who salvaged the building's frame and moved the structure about two hundred feet to a new site, replacing canvas walls with wood, and otherwise making sturdier and more attractive the theatre they would rename the Tehama.[3] Atwater traveled to Sacramento early in March to make preparations for the new company and leased the Tehama, apparently with Wingerd's financial backing. Kirby and Atwater launched their management on 25 March 1850 with another presentation of *The Lady of Lyons* and William Bernard's farce *Dumb Belle; or, The Way to Win a Husband*. Their small company included Mr. and Mrs. John Hambleton, Mr. and Mrs. Francis Nesbitt McCron, Tench Fairchild, H. F. Daly, C. E. Bingham, W. S. Fury, Sophie Edwin, Mrs. Lynes, and Mr. Alexander. Mrs. Kirby's role as a comanager was mentioned in the press, but not consistently, for it seems that in California a woman, unlike a man, had to be a solo manager before her efforts were acknowledged.[4]

Leaving the variety format at Rowe's, Kirby and Atwater chose to present a rather heavy season of old favorites including *Othello*, *Richard III*, *The Rent Day*, *The Iron Chest*, *The Wife*, and *Don Caesar de Bazan*, indicating their intention to make their theatre a serious, respectable enterprise. To encourage respectable women to attend their theatre, they enlarged the space reserved for private accommodations, and to demonstrate their concern for the local community, they gave performances to benefit such charities as the Odd Fellows and Masons Hospital. After only a month, however, the managers were faced with a significant rival establishment: the Pacific Theatre built by A. P. Petit and James Queen and opened with a grand soiree at the end of April 1850.[5]   As soon as the managers of the Tehama learned of the construction of the Pacific, they responded by remodeling their own theatre, enlarging the stage, building new scenery, and hiring more actors, including Thomas S. Campbell, who was also a talented scene painter. Rowe took the lease to the Pacific, but before he could open the beautiful new theatre, Atwater and Kirby demonstrated the improved scenic capacities of the Tehama with a spectacular piece, *The Bear Hunters*. The Tehama's first season lasted through 27 May 1850. Some members of the company then went on a tour of the interior, while the rest played a short summer season at the Tehama in June and early July.

After the summer season Atwater went back east in search of more actors, costumes, and scripts, and Sarah Kirby acted with a company led by Charles R. Thorne at the Tehama through 8 August. She also made a short trip to San Francisco to hire actors for the next season. When Thorne assumed the management of the Pacific and Atwater did not return, Kirby announced her own plans to manage a company at the Tehama. One of her first acts was to hire many actors from Thorne's Pacific company, which disbanded at the end of August. Among them was the tragedian James Stark, who assumed the leading male roles and soon joined Kirby as comanager, reopening the theatre on 9 September 1850 with that continual favorite, *The Lady of Lyons*.

During the fall the company presented a number of Shakespearean productions, including *Hamlet*, *Much Ado about Nothing*, *Othello*, *The Merchant of Venice*, *Macbeth*, and *Richard III*, as well as Otway's *Venice Preserved*, Knowles's *Virginius*, Massinger's *A New Way to Pay Old Debts*, and Payne's *Brutus*. Demonstrating their civic-mindedness, Kirby and Stark held a benefit on 27 September 1850 for the many California immigrants who had come to seek their fortune, but found themselves destitute and stranded. It was an impressive start for the new partners during their first few weeks. According to the local paper:

The Tehama Theatre, under the management of Mr. Stark and Mrs. Kirby, is a well appointed and admirably regulated establishment, with as good a company as the generality of the theatres in the United States can boast. It is really surprising that in so new a country where the profession have [*sic*] so little chance of supplying themselves with the necessary theatrical paraphanalia [*sic*], plays can so well be put upon the stage. Plays in the higher range of the Drama are nightly produced in this theatre, in a style that ought to bring an overwhelming patronage.[6]

Unfortunately, an event all too frequent in the American theatre forced the Tehama to an early close on 2 November 1850: a cholera epidemic.

At the same time cases of cholera were reported in San Francisco, though not in great enough numbers to prompt a ban on public assemblies. Kirby and Stark lost no time moving their company to San Francisco, where they leased Thomas Maguire's new Jenny Lind Theatre and opened on 4 November. The *Alta California* reported, "They have engaged probably the most efficient company procurable in California aside from their own individual merits."[7] The company began presenting many of the pieces they had played in Sacramento, but the season was interrupted when Sarah Kirby's husband, Mr. Wingerd, who had served as treasurer of the organization, died in a riding accident on 17 November. The theatre was closed for a brief period of mourning until 25 November, during which time the practical managers had a bit of remodeling done. When the theatre reopened, mostly Shakespeare and melodrama filled the bills, but on 10 January 1851 a local-interest piece, *Gold Diggers of 1750; or, The Ancient Miners of California*, was presented.

Another death, the suicide of the company's second leading lady, Mrs. Hambleton, was coupled with an attempted suicide by the object of her extramarital affections, fellow company member Mr. Coad. This behind-the-scenes drama forced the theatre to close on 14 and 15 January 1851. While the suicide of an actor was not terribly unusual, the loss of performers during those early days of the California theatre created a particular hardship for the managers, as replacements were not readily available. Mr. Hambleton further complicated the situation by blaming Sarah Kirby for the tragedy. Perhaps hoping to play to public perceptions that actresses were often immoral, Hambleton asserted that Kirby had encouraged his wife to have an affair. In a sworn statement published in the local papers, Kirby reported that Mrs. Hambleton had complained repeatedly of suffering physical abuse from her husband.[8] At one point she even asked to stay at Kirby's home. Responding in a manner apparently considered womanly and appropriate in that day, she had counseled Mrs. Hambleton to return to her husband. Sarah Kirby also revealed that she had always disliked Hambleton, but with the limited number of good actors available, she was compelled to hire him. Hambleton's supporters were unsuccessful in their attempt to disrupt the reopening performance on 16 January, as the community already held Kirby in high esteem, and the majority believed her innocence in the affair.[9]

Due to the Hambleton incident, which according to the *Alta California* "depriv[ed] them of the services of two low comedians, a leading actor and actress," the company was especially short of men.[10] This actor shortage prompted another company member, Madame Duprez, to attempt suicide after making attacks on Kirby for making her perform in a few breeches roles.[11] This was not such an unusual assignment, as Kirby herself had played in breeches on occasion. Still, Madame Duprez apparently considered breeches beneath her dignity or, perhaps, hoped to manipulate public sympathy. Such were the trials of management, with every personal difficulty covered in detail by the press.

As the cholera threat subsided in February 1851, Kirby and Stark announced their intention to return to the Tehama in Sacramento once necessary repairs were made. First they visited Stockton, playing at the new El Placer Theatre for over a week in late February. They also made plans for a new and larger theatre to be built for them in San Francisco. Finally, on 18 March 1851, Kirby and Stark reopened the Tehama. Sacramentans were happy to welcome them back in familiar plays and in newer offerings, such as the first California production of Boucicault's *London Assurance* and *Mose in Sacramento*, possibly a version of the Frank Chanfrau vehicle *Mose in California* by William Chapman.[12]

The managers were doing quite well financially, and in addition to commissioning the construction of a San Francisco theatre, they spent several thousand dollars of their own money on renovations at the Tehama.[13] Unfortunately, on 8 May 1851 they learned that their new San Francisco theatre was one of many buildings destroyed in a large fire. The managers of the new Dramatic Museum, Doc Robinson and James Evrard, who lost everything in the same fire, were given a benefit on 15 May by the Tehama company. It was not long before Doc Robinson had the opportunity to return the favor. He offered Kirby and Stark a benefit after the Tehama Theatre burned to the ground, bringing the Sacramento season to a sudden end on 14 August 1851.

Between major fires, the other big event of the 1851 season for managers Kirby and Stark was their marriage on 14 June.[14] After the legal union, Sarah Kirby changed her stage name to Sarah Stark, and James Stark was more frequently given all the credit for the couple's management, though Sarah maintained her full share of responsibility. In fact, over the years Sarah Stark proved to be the more reliable partner, as James Stark's drinking problems increased.

After losing the Tehama Theatre, the Starks did not return to management for several months because, it seems, they lacked both an available theatre and the necessary capital. Disbanding their Sacramento company, the Starks sought acting jobs in San Francisco. The couple joined Doc Robinson's company on 20 October 1851 at the new American, a theatre that settled three inches into the mud during the opening night performance. The Starks' engagement at the American lasted only about a month before young Charlie Robinson, appearing in one scene with Sarah Stark in *The Stranger*, sparked a feud. Awakened by his mother just before his entrance, the tired and confused boy cursed Sarah

Stark, provoking the audience to laugh during the emotional climax of the melodramatic play. Publicly humiliated, Sarah Stark was convinced that Mrs. Robinson had coached her son in this behavior. Her reaction to a seemingly minor incident suggests her frustration at no longer controlling her own theatre. The episode prompted the Starks to leave the American and join Junius Brutus Booth's company at the [third] Jenny Lind Theatre, from 8 December 1851 to 20 January 1852.

Next the Starks played a short engagement at the Adelphi, before acquiring the lease to the American and once again organizing their own company, with the assistance of James Evrard, to play there beginning in late April 1852. James Stark appeared infrequently with the new company, taking a farewell benefit on 17 June before heading east, while Sarah Stark continued to perform at the American through September. Stark returned to California in December, and the couple chose to give up management for a time in order to try to earn their fortune by touring Australia.[15] Leaving in early 1853 the Starks found eager audiences and did not return to San Francisco until July 1854, after reportedly earning over $100,000.[16]

Unfortunately, the Starks had lost their preeminent position among California performers during their travels and also had difficulty reestablishing themselves as managers. They played a number of engagements, though without their previous popularity, and in the fall of 1855 James Stark managed a season at the Union Theatre, San Francisco, under his name, sharing the bill with unusual acts such as ropewalkers. On 13 January 1856 Sarah Stark took up the lease of the Union with Mrs. Woodward as her comanager. Edmond Gagey reports, "Their advertisements carried a running caption 'The Old Folks at Home,' but despite the domestic and reminiscent approach the venture did not prosper."[17] Sarah Stark soon took a farewell benefit, turned her share in the partnership over to a Miss Goodard, and with her husband returned to Australia.

The Starks were not successful on their second Australian tour, and they returned to California in May 1857 and soon left for the East, playing a short engagement at Wallack's, New York, in April 1858. Over the next few years they played a number of engagements in California, Nevada, and Oregon, including twenty nights in October 1859 when they opened the first theatre in San Jose, which had been named in their honor. Early in the 1860s James Stark retired from acting for three years to spend his time silver mining, but Sarah continued on the stage. Apparently always happy to manage a theatre when she had the chance, she leased the Metropolitan, San Francisco, with actress Emily Jordan and presented a season from 25 December 1863 to 19 March 1864. Their management included Saturday matinees for women and children and featured a guest appearance by Julia Dean Hayne.

In 1868 Sarah Stark finally divorced her increasingly irresponsible husband, who ended his career playing bit parts with Edwin Booth in New York before he died on 12 October 1875. After receiving a benefit at the San

Francisco Opera House in 1869, Sarah Stark traveled east and married a Dr. Gray of New York. Following his death, she married her old friend actor-manager Charles R. Thorne, whom she had outlived by five years when she died in 1898. Sarah Stark's obituary in the *New York Dramatic Mirror* noted, "She was a very clever actress, and had considerable business ability, especially in the field of theatrical management, having managed various companies and theatres in California and elsewhere with marked success."[18]

One of the earliest managers and certainly the first woman manager in California, Sarah Kirby Stark had an important role in establishing the legitimate theatre in the territory. Including Shakespeare and other classics in her repertory, even during the early days of playing under rather crude conditions for audiences of miners, Sarah Stark set a high standard for those who followed. Between 1850 and 1864 she was involved in the management of five different theatres in Sacramento and San Francisco. Her four comanagers included two women, a clear indication that she considered women to be competent managers. Sarah Stark's managerial partnerships demonstrate a collaborative approach to theatrical enterprises, rather than lack of individual initiative, and she is acknowledged in contemporary newspaper accounts as a full-fledged manager, not just another manager's assistant. Further, Sarah Stark had arranged to manage the Tehama on her own in 1850 before she developed a fortunate partnership with James Stark, which provided her with a good leading man and, eventually, a husband. An enterprising woman who was able to adapt to a variety of circumstances, from the crudest early California theatres to their more sophisticated replacements, she weathered the adversity that eventually broke the spirit of her husband, six years her junior. She is remembered as a true pioneer of the theatre in California.

CATHERINE SINCLAIR

Catherine Norton Sinclair was another noteworthy woman who became a theatre manager in California following the discovery of gold. The daughter of vocalist John Sinclair, Catherine was born near London in 1818. Married to Edwin Forrest in 1837, she did not prepare for a stage career of her own until her impending divorce made it clear that she would have to support herself. Though Sinclair was legally separated from Forrest by March 1849, the highly publicized divorce trial did not end until 24 January 1852, when a decision was made in her favor. However, Sinclair did not soon see the $3,000 per year in alimony payments, as Forrest kept the case in appeals for sixteen years, and when a final decision in 1868 awarded her $64,000, most of that amount had already been spent in legal fees. Meanwhile, Sinclair determined to make the most of her notoriety, and after being coached by actor George Vandenhoff, she made her stage debut as Lady Teazle in *The School for Scandal* at Brougham's Lyceum, New York, on 2 February 1852. Her engagement lasted five weeks, and while no one was overly impressed by her acting ability, curious crowds made the run profitable. Sinclair then set out on a tour of American cities, apparently making some improvement as she gained experience. She arrived in California in early May 1853, and played several engagements in San Francisco, Sacramento, and Marysville before making her managerial debut.

On 24 December 1853 San Francisco's magnificent new Metropolitan Theatre, built as part of a larger development project by architect Joseph Trench, opened under the management of Catherine Sinclair with a performance of *The School for Scandal*.[19]   Sinclair's evident plan was to present lavish productions to draw a first-class audience to her 2,200-seat theatre.   Though California audiences were more appreciative of Sinclair's acting than audiences in other parts of the country, Sinclair wisely decided not to depend on her own ability as leading lady in her new venture. Instead, she hired a strong stock company of regulars on the California stage including Mrs. Judah, Mrs. Woodward, Miss Montague, Miss Julia Gould, and Messrs. Anderson, Barry, McGowan, Wilder, E. Booth, and J. B. Booth, who also served as stage manager during the first season. She booked a number of visiting stars as well. Actors who played at the Metropolitan during Sinclair's reign were James Murdoch, the Irish comedian Mr. Hudson, Matilda Heron, Laura Keene, the Bateman children, Mr. and Mrs. Barney Williams, Caroline and William Chapman, Mr. and Mrs. James Stark, and Jean Davenport, with popular performers, such as the Batemans and the Williamses, frequently reengaged.

In addition to her dramatic offerings Sinclair produced opera, ballet, and other musical attractions. Not a last-ditch effort to save her management, the opera series was part of Sinclair's ambitions from the beginning, with the upcoming engagement of the first guest opera star, Madame Anna Thillon, announced on opening night. Thillon first appeared on 18 January 1854, singing every other night through 8 February, usually in English, in operas such as *Crown Diamonds*, *Daughter of the Regiment*, and *Black Domino*. She also made several more appearances over the next three months. Like the other opera singers who would perform at the Metropolitan, Thillon was supported by a small number of professional singers, by members of the dramatic company who could sing, and by a chorus of mostly amateurs, hired and trained for the occasion. Sinclair engaged Madame Anna Bishop for a series of operas beginning 30 April 1854, and from 14 November 1854 presented the Italian Opera Troupe, featuring Madame Thorn. On several occasions during Sinclair's management Mrs. Margaret Voorhees, Sinclair's sister, was a featured singer in one of the musical presentations. Despite the opportunity to promote her sister, Sinclair's emphasis on opera was a rather curious choice, as her sister was not popular enough to be a starred performer and Sinclair herself did not sing. Her one attempt at a singing role took place on 25 November 1854, months after she began presenting opera, and when she was not well received, Sinclair gracefully withdrew after a single performance. In addition to opera Sinclair presented dance, with the Monplaisir troupe making regular appearances for several months, sometimes presenting elaborate evening-long ballets or spectacular pantomimes, assisted by members of the dramatic company, and other times providing a dance that was one act on a multiple bill.

In producing such a variety of entertainment, Sinclair bore the costs of magnificent scenery for the operas and ballets, the expense of maintaining a double company for dramatic and musical productions, and the high fees demanded by stars, especially operatic stars. The *Spirit of the Times* judged that her payments to stars showed "a degree of liberality on the part of Mrs. Sinclair, in providing entertainments for the San Francisco public, beyond parallel in the history of the drama."[20] Introducing opera to local audiences and developing their taste for spectacular productions was an expensive gamble on Sinclair's part, but at first it seemed to pay, as eager audiences packed the theatre. However, San Francisco's economy was in a recession and had suffered a panic in February 1855, prompting local residents to become more cautious in spending money on entertainment.[21] Trying to draw an audience, Sinclair continued to produce new attractions in the same lavish manner, but began to have trouble meeting expenses. She also had difficulty retaining dramatic actors who sought greater opportunities at theatres where they did not have to share time with opera singers. Unfortunately, Sinclair's finances dwindled to the point that she was unable to make full payments to the opera stars but needed them to perform in order to raise the additional sums. Finally, on 3 May 1855, the Italian Opera Troupe, seeing a small house and fearing they would not be paid, refused to perform. Sinclair appeared before the audience and said:

> The artists composing the Italian Opera Troupe positively refuse to sing in consequence of the insufficiency of the attendance here this evening, and I have assumed the unpleasant task of making this statement in order to exonerate myself from any charge of willingly disappointing the public whom I have so long and diligently served. Since I have assumed the management of this theatre, it has been a matter more of pride than of profit to me to present to the public the greatest attractions I could possibly procure: I have used my utmost endeavors to produce the Italian opera with every accessory which the country could furnish, and it is my misfortune that the expenditure has not been justified by the receipts; the latter being in accordance with the depressed state of the times, the former with the demands of the artists. Having hitherto sustained heavy losses from the representations of opera, I did not propose again to undertake them, except upon the assurance of an ample subscription, which had unfortunately not been made up, but when I found the artists had

bestowed much time on the study and preparation of *I Lombardi*, I was induced to set aside more profitable and less expensive attractions for their accommodation.[22]

By 7 May cards from the Italian Opera Troupe were published in the local papers reporting that Sinclair had profited and not paid them for their work. This led Sinclair to reveal the finances of two previous series of sixteen operas by the Italian Troupe, on which she had lost first $3,908 and then $9,877.[23]

The Italian opera debacle signaled the approaching end of Sinclair's management. The Metropolitan was closed for a few nights during the week of 7 May for cleaning, reopening from 14 to 21 May with a ballet program, followed by Miss Davenport's farewell engagement, which, faced with dwindling attendance, closed on 7 June. A farewell benefit for Sinclair with a long program including *The School for Scandal* was announced for 9 June 1855. Urging the public to attend the benefit the *Alta California* reported that

quite a number of persons have made fortunes at this theatre and gone away to other parts to spend them. The management, however, has been on too liberal a scale to leave anything for her who has conducted it. At a time when theatres were profitable, inducements were held out that brought to California nearly all the leading stars in the country, so that the people of San Francisco have been favored with theatrical and operatic entertainments equal to those of any city in the United States. Other managers may be more successful pecuniarily, but it will be very long before another will make such exertions and incur such expense to put upon the boards so superior and expensive entertainments.[24]

Despite her admirable exertions, after two seasons, or about eighteen months, Sinclair had little choice but to give up the management of the Metropolitan Theatre. In retrospect her San Francisco management can be seen as her greatest theatrical achievement. Although Sinclair was only a mediocre actress, she was an inspired manager who worked hard to raise the standards of theatrical production on the West Coast. She continued to perform in California, managing a short season on a more modest scale at the Sacramento Theatre in the fall of 1855, and she received another farewell benefit on 15 March 1856, before leaving for Australia. After she toured Australia, she performed in England and then returned to New York, where she gave her last public performance in December 1859, and lived in retirement until her death in 1891.

LAURA KEENE AND MRS. JOHN WOOD

Two other women, Laura Keene and Mrs. John Wood, who would both
earn greater recognition as managers of theatres in New York City, acquired
early managerial experience in California. Laura Keene, who had launched her
first managerial effort in Baltimore on 24 December 1853, the same night that
Sinclair opened the Metropolitan, abandoned her Baltimore theatre within three
months and traveled west, making her California debut with a three-night
engagement at Sinclair's theatre on 6–8 April 1854.[25] Next, Keene made a
quick tour of Sacramento, Marysville, and Stockton, before becoming sole
manager and lessee of the Union Theatre in San Francisco. She attempted to
attract an audience by producing light comic pieces. Typical of her fare was
Doc Robinson's *The Prize; or, $1,000 in a Horn*, which burlesqued the
Bateman family, who had selected Mrs. Bateman's *A Mother's Trust; or,
California in 1849* as winner of their own prize-play contest. Another piece
produced by Keene was *The Camp at the Union*, a local extravaganza which
included imitations of other California performers. Keene also made a big hit
at the Union with a production of the spectacular melodrama *The Sea of Ice;
or, The Orphan of the Sea*, a play she later revived in New York with great
success.

At this point in her career, Keene's greatest deficiency as a manager was
an apparent tendency to abandon projects prematurely. Early in August 1854
she suddenly abandoned her management of the Union and left for a tour of
Australia with Edwin Booth and D. C. Anderson. As the Union reportedly
was still drawing crowds, there was no readily discernible reason for Keene to
remove herself from the profitable situation. The *Spirit of the Times*, published
in New York where many theatregoers remembered her unexpected departure
from Wallack's Theatre during the previous year, criticized Keene at length,
warned her against ruining her good name in the profession, and wondered if
she was merely seeking notoriety.[26] Keene's real motivation in making the
trip, however, seems to have been to locate and obtain a divorce from her
husband, John Taylor, an English convict who had reportedly been exiled to
Australia.

Returning to San Francisco in the spring of 1855, Keene may have leased
the American Theatre, where from May to early August she was involved in
the production of several plays, including *Twelfth Night*, *A Midsummer Night's
Dream*, and *The Tempest*, which were all admired for their beautiful
scenery.[27] Though not as greatly appreciated as an actress in California as
she had been in New York, Keene did receive recognition for careful attention
to production elements, a trait she would further develop in her managerial
career.[28] Although she had managed theatres in California (and before that
in Baltimore) for only a few months, Keene nevertheless began to acquire
familiarity with the duties of a theatre manager and the business details of
operating a theatre. She gained valuable experience working with actors and

mounting productions, mostly comedies, that prepared her to establish herself as an important manager in New York City the following winter. Most importantly, it seems that after these brief managerial stints, Keene realized that success in the theatre required some perseverance. She returned to New York apparently resolved not to look for a different project when faced with difficulty, but to overcome any obstacles she faced.

Mrs. John (Matilda Vining) Wood also gained managerial experience in California before making her name as a New York theatre manager. An English actress who came to the United States with her husband in 1854, Mrs. Wood excelled in musical comedy and burlesque and soon became more popular than Mr. Wood. The Woods' first California engagement began 18 January 1858 at Maguire's Opera House, San Francisco, and lasted forty-four nights, after which they played in other towns.[29] In the summer of 1858 the couple separated before an eventual divorce and stopped acting together. In February 1859 Mrs. Wood was briefly the manager of the Forrest Theatre, Sacramento, and in March and early April she was manager of the American Theatre, San Francisco.[30] At both theatres she presented pieces such as *Pocahontas* and *Actress by Daylight*, which were regular features in her repertory as she toured the country for the next five years. While Wood's management is fairly insignificant in the history of California theatricals, the experience of being a lessee of two theatres, in addition to managing a traveling company, undoubtedly gave her confidence when she entered the managerial arena in New York in 1863. Coincidentally, the house Wood leased at that time and converted into the Olympic was none other than Laura Keene's Theatre, relinquished by Keene when she returned to touring.

ROWENA GRANICE

The California theatre management activities of Keene and Wood are of interest primarily because of their later achievements as managers of first-class New York theatres. Rowena Granice, on the other hand, reached her managerial apex in California at a theatre that was never mistaken for a first-class house. Granice's theatre, The Gaieties, Temple of Mirth and Song, bore a grand name but was actually a "bit" theatre, catering to a rambunctious male audience.[31] However, Granice demonstrated as much energy and determination as any of the other women, in addition to a great deal of nerve in playing with limited resources for a difficult audience. Granice, born in New York on 20 June 1824 and married to Thomas Claughley in 1846, had arrived in California in 1856 with her two sons in pursuit of the husband who had abandoned the family in 1853. Finding Claughley, who proved to be something of a bum, Granice dropped his name and supported her sons by tending bar and writing fiction.[32] She soon established the Gaieties, located at 77 Long Wharf, San Francisco, in a building that had been built to house a publishing business. Starring herself in the productions, Granice was supported by whatever combination of out-of-luck professionals and eager amateurs she could round up, often casting boys in women's roles.[33] The actors sat around tables with the audience, making entrances from the house and helping to change the sets in the tiny theatre with a narrow gallery on three sides. A writer who visited the Gaieties, T. S. Kenderdine, recalled, "It was of no greater pretensions than scores of the rickety buildings surrounding it, except that it was two stories. The bar-room was as prominent a part of the premises as the liquor announcement was of the posters, as the audience was forced to pass through it to get to the 'auditorium.' "[34]

Precise dates for Granice's management are not known, as she relied on posters and word of mouth, rather than newspaper advertisements. The Gaieties apparently opened sometime in 1856, as Lotta Crabtree reportedly made one of her earliest appearances, singing between the acts at the Gaieties during that year.[35] Granice, herself, in a letter to the *Daily Evening Bulletin*, wrote that she had opened the Gaieties in the spring of 1859, although it seems that she had actually reopened the theatre after an extended absence, during which she had performed in a theatre in Sacramento.[36] The success of the venture provoked the jealousy of Claughley, who tried to gain control of the theatre and, failing in that, boarded the doors shut, despite the fact that he was dependent on his wife's income. On 10 August 1859 the *Daily Evening Bulletin* reported:

> A "scene" occurred at the Gaieties Theatre to-day. Miss Rowena Granice, the sole lessee and proprietor, was in peaceable possession. Mr. Thomas Claughley last night closed and nailed it up. Miss Rowena Granice this morning opened it. Mr. Claughley closed it a second time and Miss Rowena Granice opened it a second time, and kept it open. During the above play of "dead open and shut," Mr. Claughley and Miss Granice were arrested, at each other's complaint, for malicious mischief; and the chorus was performed by the crowd, who shouted: "Hurra for crinoline!" Miss Granice seems to be persecuted by Claughley; but if she be left alone, she will soon get the better of him.[37]

Despite this brave stand, Granice was not truly in control of the Gaieties, for Claughley was helping himself to the profits. Explaining her position in a letter published in the *Daily Evening Bulletin*, Granice stated that she had received a small loan from Claughley in order to open her business. The initial receipts of the house were turned over to Claughley, who continued to pocket the proceeds long after the debt was repaid. When Granice finally thought she would see some of the profits of her regularly crowded theatre, Claughley had come up with a new scheme:

[I]n want of a few hundreds, and as the place was worth about $1,500, he conceived the happy idea of selling out and pocketing the proceeds. In order to do this, he would have to make the situation disagreeable to me, and how well he succeeded is well known. I was driven from the establishment, without a dollar, for four months' hard mental and physical labor. After being absent for two weeks, during which time he found he could not sell out and that business was not paying, he called at my residence and solicited my return to the Gaieties; and as I had two little ones depending upon me for bread, and no prospect of other business, I consented. But I soon found that the arrangement was only a scheme to improve the house for the benefit of parties who had previously leased it, and the third day I was locked out. I fought bravely for what I considered my rights for two days, but found the parties had the advantage of me in numbers—six vulgar men against one woman was more than I could stand—and having no money to fee a lawyer, I concluded to give them possession.[38]

While Granice never refers to Claughley as her estranged husband, her ambitions were apparently defeated by the right of a husband to his wife's property and wages, combined with physical intimidation.

From 13 August to 15 September 1859 an advertisement in the *Daily Evening Bulletin* announced the presence of a new stock company at the former Gaieties, renamed the Varieties. It seems Granice resumed management of the theatre after this company disappeared. Whether Claughley was still around and attempting to control the theatre is not known. On 23 December 1859 Lotta returned and gave a benefit performance as Topsy in *Uncle Tom's Cabin* for Granice, who had earlier helped her secure an engagement at the Forrest Theatre, Sacramento.[39] The Varieties had become rather run-down by this point, as had the neighborhood where it was located, and Granice did not keep the theatre open long past this night. Though this marked the end of her theatre career, it was not the end of public activity by the energetic Granice. Marrying newspaper owner Robert J. Steele in 1861 after Claughley's death, Granice took up newspaper writing, editing, and publishing with her husband and sons.[40] In her later years before her death in 1881, Granice was a temperance worker and advocate of women's suffrage.[41]

These early women theatre managers in California seized the opportunity presented by a marked increase in the amusement-seeking public in the territory, a result of the Gold Rush. The entertainments they produced ranged from Granice's low-priced, hastily and somewhat haphazardly produced offerings to Sinclair's upscale, lavish operas, with Stark bridging the gap during her years as an actress-manager. Stark began her California career playing under fairly crude conditions to audiences of miners, but she aimed high, presenting the standard fare with as much dignity as circumstances would permit. Sinclair developed the trend toward high culture, presenting opera and ballet with lavish scenery in her beautiful new theatre. Granice's management, on the other hand, met a continuing demand for low-brow entertainment. While Stark, Sinclair, and Granice made their mark as California theatre managers, Keene and Wood used short stints as managers in California to gain practical experience in the operation of a theatre before beginning more noted management careers in New York. Considered as a group, these women were quite active in theatre management in California during the 1850s and were unhindered by any noticeable opposition to women in such positions. Granice was the only woman among this group to face serious male challenge in running her theatre, and this seems to have been a matter of personal jealousy and greed on the part of her husband rather than an ideological objection to tolerating a woman in a position of power.

At this time women moved into more prominent roles as managers than they had previously held in the United States. Women managers were no longer found only in small or inherited theatres. No longer an isolated example, a woman manager was not an oddity in California. The activities of women managers even received occasional notice back East, in the New York newspapers. After the California developments, the next step would be for Keene to challenge the male managerial establishment directly in the major theatrical city, New York.

NOTES

1. See Jacqueline Baker Barnhart, *The Fair but Frail: Prostitution in San Francisco 1849–1900* (Reno: University of Nevada Press, 1986), for more information on the opportunity some women found to move into managerial roles in the prostitution business.

2. See Douglas McDermott, "Touring Patterns on California's Theatrical Frontier, 1849–1859," *Theatre Survey* 15 (May 1974): 18–28, for more on theatrical routes during the period.

3. Charles Vernard Hume, "The Sacramento Theatre 1849–1885" (Ph.D. diss., Stanford University, 1955), 53.

4. This point is raised in Marjorie R. Whitehead, "Sarah Kirby Stark: California's Pioneer Actress-Manager" (Master's thesis, California State University at Sacramento, 1972), 4–5.

5. Ibid., 28–9.

6. *Sacramento Transcript*, 16 October 1850, quoted in ibid., 55.

7. *Alta California*, 4 November 1850, [2].

8. Ibid., 16 January 1851, [2].

9. Ibid., 17 January 1851, [2].

10. Ibid.

11. Whitehead, 75.

12. Kirby and Stark's company had presented the original Mose play, Benjamin Baker's *A Glance at New York*, in December 1850, and a Mose play with California local color would have had a special appeal for their audiences.

13. Whitehead, 99. In addition to being a manager, Sarah Kirby became a theatre proprietor during the spring of 1851, apparently purchasing the Tehama, according to Hume, 84.

14. *Alta California*, 19 June 1851, [2].

15. Many gold seeking entertainers ventured on to Australia from California. See Harold Love, ed., *The Australian Stage: A Documentary History* (Kensington NSW, Australia: New South Wales University Press, 1984), 55.

16. *San Francisco Theatre Research Monographs* (W.P.A. Project 1938–42) 3:18.

17. Edmond M. Gagey, *The San Francisco Stage* (New York: Columbia University Press, 1950), 41.

18. *New York Dramatic Mirror*, 17 December 1898, 13.

19. *San Francisco Theatre Research Monographs* 15:135.

20. *Spirit of the Times*, 3 February 1855, 608.

21. Roger W. Lotchin, *San Francisco 1846–1856: From Hamlet to City* (New York: Oxford University Press, 1974), 59.

22. *Alta California*, 4 May 1855, [2].

23. Ibid., 9 May 1855, [2]. The treasurer's statement printed in the newspaper contains a list of receipts and special expenses for the opera series. The information appears reasonably consistent with financial information published in the *Spirit of the Times*, 3 February 1855 (information reportedly taken from the *Golden Era*). The article included a list of receipts for selected first night and entire weeks of engagements.

24. *Alta California*, 9 June 1855, [2].

25. Positive notices in the *Sun* (Baltimore) give no indication why Keene decided to end her management of the Charles Street Theatre. Presumably, she was attracted by the rumor of large sums to be earned by performers in California.

26. *Spirit of the Times*, 16 September 1854, 362.

27. The *Spirit of the Times* stated that Keene was manager of the American, and Edmond Gagey repeats this assertion. Walter Leman, in *Memories of an Old Actor* (San Francisco: A. Roman Company, 1886), 250, recalled that Keene became the stage manager, while George MacMinn in *The Theatre of the Golden Era in California* (Caldwell, Idaho: Caxton Printers Ltd., 1941), 91, says she was the "producing star." Dorothy Jean Taylor, in "Laura Keene in America, 1852–73" (Ph.D. diss., Tulane University, 1966), 76, also states that Keene became a manager of the theatre. Advertisements for the American in the *Alta California* name first Volney Spalding, then James Dowling as manager of the American during this period—not Keene, though

with her name in all capital letters she was clearly the star. Although her exact responsibilities are not known, it seems clear that Keene had some involvement in the management of the American Theatre while she starred there.

28. Praise for the scenic elements of Keene's Shakespearean productions in San Francisco, excerpted from local papers, can be found in MacMinn. About *A Midsummer Night's Dream* the reviewer for the *Pioneer* wrote, "The rising moon, the flowing water, which seemed to stretch far back among and under the trees, the flowers opening upon the stage to let Puck out, and to display the fairies, the green banks, woodland glade, spirits—all were admirable"(quoted in MacMinn, 91).

29. Gagey, 94-95.

30. Barnard Hewitt entry on Mrs. Wood in Edward T. James, ed., *Notable American Women 1607-1950: A Biographical Dictionary*, 3 vols. (Cambridge: Belknap Press of Harvard University, 1971), 648-49, and the *Daily Evening Bulletin* (San Francisco), 9 April 1859, [1].

31. A "bit" theatre was an inexpensive place of amusement with the typical admission price of twelve and a half cents, or one bit. In the *San Francisco Theatre Research Monographs* 15:215, the Gaieties is also referred to as a melodeon.

32. In 1858 Granice published *The Family Gem: Miscellaneous Stories*, a short work containing stories previously published in journals. Her 1860 novel *Victims of Fate* reportedly sold five thousand copies. Her later novels included *Leonie St. James; or, The Suicide's Curse, Dell Dart; or, Within the Meshes*, and *Weak or Wicked?* (all published under the name Rowena Granice Steele); MacMinn, 185-90. In the introduction to *The Family Gem* Granice claims that her stories are fact, not fiction, and were written "amidst the duties of the stage and the tearful realities of domestic desolation." The lead story, "The Two Wives," concerns a man who leaves his wife and two small sons in the East, travels to California, and takes a new wife; *The Family Gem; Miscellaneous Stories* (Sacramento, Calif.: Old State University Steam Presses, 1858).

33. Dolores Waldorf Bryant, "No. 77 Long Wharf: From Publishing Hall to Temple of Mirth," *California Historical Society Quarterly* 21 (March 1942): 77.

34. T. S. Kenderdine, *A California Tramp* (1859), quoted in *San Francisco Theatre Research Monographs* 15:183-84.

35. Constance Rourke, *Troupers of the Gold Coast, or the Rise of Lotta Crabtree* (New York: Harcourt, Brace and Company, 1928), and Bryant, 77-78.

36. *Daily Evening Bulletin* (San Francisco), 13 August 1859, [3].

37. Ibid., 10 August 1859, [3].

38. Ibid., 13 August 1859, [3].

39. Rourke, 143.

40. R. Dean Galloway, "Merced Newspapers; A History 1862-64," 2

parts of *Acquisitions List Stanislaus State College Library* 6 (June and July 1967). In Rowena Granice clipping file, Billy Rose Theatre Collection, New York Public Library at Lincoln Center.

41. Granice apparently did not advertise regularly in the local papers; therefore, a complete record of her seasons is not available. No advertisements or notices of her activities during the fall of 1856 appear in either the *Alta California* or the *Daily Evening Bulletin* (San Francisco).   The only advertisements which appeared in 1859 were an announcement of the change in name from the Gaieties to the Varieties and change of management (no names given), which ran for the first two weeks in September 1859 in the *Bulletin*, and an advertisement for Granice's benefit featuring Lotta, which appeared on 23 and 24 December 1859 in the *Bulletin*.

3

Laura Keene—First-Class Theatre Manager in New York City

As demonstrated in the previous chapters, Laura Keene was not the first woman to manage a theatre in the United States. Her managerial career, however, made a great impact on the New York theatrical scene, and she brought widespread recognition to the existence of "lady managers" or "fair manageresses." While other women had earlier managed theatres in New York, Keene was the first to control a large, first-class house and to compete in the same league with established male managers. Following her advent as manager, women who chose to pursue a management career increasingly were viewed by their contemporaries as part of a tradition, unlike earlier women managers who often appeared as isolated anomalies. Keene's success for eight years as a New York theatre manager, a more significant factor in her lasting reputation than was her acting ability, could be pointed to by later managerial hopefuls as evidence that a woman could operate a theatre as well as a man. But since she was the first to achieve such a degree of ascendancy, she had to bear the brunt of opposition against women in theatre management.

Not only the grand scale of her ambitions, but the timing of her career caused some difficulties for Keene. Besides the problems of the period shared by all managers, such as the financial panic of 1857 and the beginning of the Civil War, Keene had to contend with the great debate taking shape over the proper role of women in American society. Women were making advances in areas such as education and employment opportunities. However, as some became more vocal in their demands for liberties enjoyed by American men, they stirred up opposition from both men and women who preferred to maintain the status quo. As Keene attempted to establish herself as a theatre manager in New York in 1855, the implications of her actions, running a competitive business and supervising male employees, were seen by many as a direct challenge to the existing social order. Furthermore, her own choice to emphasize gender, cultivating a public persona of the persecuted woman, made her a clear example of the type of resistance women sometimes encountered as theatre managers.

Keene had first appeared before a New York audience on 20 September 1852 as Albina de Mandeville in *The Will* at Wallack's Theatre. In desperate need of a leading lady for his new theatre, James Wallack took a chance on this newcomer, whose short acting career in England included a few months with the well-known woman theatre manager Madame Vestris. With her second role at Wallack's, that of Lydia Languish in *The Rivals*, Keene proved her popularity with New York audiences and secured her position as leading lady in the company. Finding herself suddenly at the top of her profession, she had to work hard to maintain her position, and as she possessed a very slight repertoire, she had to learn at least twenty-five roles during her first season. This glorified apprenticeship served her well, as she repeated many of the roles frequently in later years. She also received special assistance and training from the elder Wallack, who undoubtedly understood that the growing success and prominence of his establishment was in some part due to Keene's popularity.

New York theatregoers were surprised by the abrupt termination of Keene's engagement at Wallack's not long into her second season. On 25 November 1853 Keene failed to arrive at the theatre for her scheduled appearance in *The Rivals*, and Lester Wallack, managing the theatre in his father's absence, informed the audience of her sudden departure without notice and fired her. Meanwhile, Keene traveled to Baltimore to investigate the possibility of opening the Charles Street Theatre, also known as the Howard Athenaeum, under her own management. She would be assisted in this undertaking by John Lutz, who had secured support from several prominent Baltimore business leaders and would serve as Keene's business manager.[1]

Quite possibly Keene had a firm intention to enter management, and the discovery of her plans only resulted in her being out of Wallack's employ a bit sooner than she expected. It may have been, however, that her firing from Wallack's cemented tentative plans to strike out on her own. Keene played a brief engagement in Boston while waiting for slight renovations to be made on the Charles Street Theatre, which she opened on 24 December 1853. Though the Baltimore venture was apparently not profitable and lasted only a couple of months, Keene had launched her career as a theatre manager. Her decision to leave Wallack's received a great deal of criticism. Some observers were troubled by her apparent ingratitude to Wallack, first deserting and later rivaling him, while others, though sympathetic to Keene's wish to manage her own theatre, pointed out that she might have had a more comfortable life if she had satisfied herself with simply acting. Joseph Ireland, reflecting on Keene's earlier career during later years when her health and acting ability were failing her, wrote:

Miss Keene made a favourable impression, and had she remained in the establishment, under the guidance of Mr. Wallack, would probably have become the most elegant and favourite *artiste* in the city. She, however, threw up the advantage of her position, and after enjoying the dubious honor of management for a few seasons, is now a wanderer in the provinces.[2]

While theatrical management was a risky endeavor compared to the relatively secure position of a leading lady in a first-class New York theatre, it offered great potential for power and profit. As a manager Keene would be able to control play selection and casting, hire all performers and staff, supervise all elements of production, and by assuming the financial risk, take a chance at gaining greater financial reward. It seems reasonable, therefore, to view Keene's decision to enter management as an ambitious choice, rather than a foolhardy mistake.

Having made the choice to be a manager and gained experience in Baltimore and San Francisco, Keene returned to New York in September 1855 to test her ambitions by opening her own theatre in America's leading theatrical city. She leased the Metropolitan at Broadway and Bond Street, renovated and renamed it Laura Keene's Varieties, and began hiring a large acting company and corps de ballet to open her theatre on 24 December 1855. As the theatrical season was already underway and the best actors presumably employed, Keene concentrated her efforts on luring actors away from other theatres, offering higher salaries or taking advantage of an actor's dissatisfaction with present employment. This was an expedient business move on Keene's part, but not one designed to make her popular with her competitors. One of the managers damaged by Keene's raids, William Burton, who had lost five actors to Keene's Baltimore company, now found George Jordan, Kate Reignolds, Fred Lyster, John Dyott, Rosalie Durand, and Mrs. Carpenter, among others, ready to desert him.[3]

A masterful publicist, Keene excited public interest in her theatre before it opened. Large advertisements, often filling twice the column inches as the ads of her competitors, would become a Laura Keene trademark, and first appeared in the *New York Herald* on 22 December 1855.[4] An article in the *Spirit of the Times* anticipated the opening of the Varieties, quoting California papers that praised Keene and regretted her departure for New York.[5] George C. D. Odell noted that the opening of Laura Keene's Varieties was "a highly important event," writing,

The great popularity of the lady during her year or more as leading actress at Wallack's, her sensational departure to assume control of the Baltimore theatre, her subsequent wanderings in California and Australia, the long absence which had made the hearts of her admirers grow fonder—all these circumstance tended to whet curiosity as to her new scheme.[6]

Not all the interest in Keene's venture was supportive. Running a theatre was a risky and difficult enterprise, and established managers naturally resented any new competition. That the new threat to their livelihood was a woman apparently provided an additional affront to at least one manager. According to Odell, E. A. Marshall, manager of the Broadway Theatre, attempting to undermine support for the woman manager, "indulged in acrimonious newspaper correspondence."[7] One anonymous example of the anti-Keene sentiment appeared in the *New York Evening Express*:

> Mrs. Laura Keene, whose disposition to have her own way, and remove every obstacle to a full sway for reaching the height of her ambition, without hindrance of managers, is about to open Mr. LaFarge's curious architectural anomaly in Broadway on her own hook. Laura, returning from an unsuccessful colonization of California, proposes to inaugurate a female theatrical management in this city. Sole manager, sole lessee, sole actress, she enters upon the ominous sphere of Mr. Willard [a previous lessee], with almost as sonorous a flourish a trumpets as that very portentious impressario....

> From some one reason or another Mr. LaFarge's wooden, iron marble building, has not proved very attractive, even under the most favorable auspices. The difficulty of getting audiences into it as a theatre, or borders in it as a hotel, would seem to be so insurmountable that the worthy projector had pretty much concluded that the public was more in want of stores and lecture rooms, than the accommodations he had provided. The happy results of this very judicious conclusion, however, have been prevented by Laura, as to the theatre, by her proposed extension of woman's rights in a female managerial experiment. It might not be a bad idea now for the proprietor to finish the other portions of his premises for free love purposes....

> [T]he depletion which her new experiment is likely to effect upon herself and her courageous backers, will, we fear, hardly give her time, even to gain her object of spiting either Burton or Wallack for not securing her talents at their establishments on her arrival here. She will not, of course, be any the poorer at the end than she was at the beginning of the affair, as her resources would appear to be of the Fortunatus' purse character. But is her undertaking to be nevertheless without evil results? Shall we give special encouragement to a scheme of bribing off at preposterous salaries the actors at other houses where the people habitually seek their entertainment, and back them up in the scoundrelly business of breaking their engagements? Shall we see these establishments hindered by erratic and malicious opposition, set on foot for temporary private spite? Shall we see worthy and

experienced managers, such as Burton and Wallack driven from our midst by persons whose efforts and influence have every tendency to break up the stage and bring it into vilest disgrace and disrepute?[8]

Whether this commentary was provided by Marshall or some other person interested in protecting the interests of the established managers, it did not offer the new manager a warm or even a civil welcome. Further describing Keene's efforts as an "Amazonian onslaught," the writer presents Keene not as a new competitor in the managerial ranks, but as a dangerous intruder.

Keene's response to these attacks demonstrated a tactic that she would use throughout her career. Criticized implicitly for being a woman in a man's world, Keene summoned her full command of wronged female virtue to condemn her critics as unchivalrous, complaining of "gratuitous and unmanly attacks," "ungenerous and unjust allusions [and] malicious insinuations."[9] Though Keene was as fiercely aggressive a competitor as any of her male rivals, she adopted an acceptably ladylike public persona as a strategy for deflecting criticism. Because the press and the public were concerned with her gender, Keene attempted not to down play her difference from the men, but to use the difference to her advantage.[10]

Keene announced the opening of the Varieties for 24 December 1855 with J. R. Planché's *Prince Charming* and an afterpiece called *Two Can Play at That Game*, a program interpreted by many as a reference to *King Charming*, Marshall's announced Christmas offering at the Broadway. A later newspaper account noted that a "quarrel ensued, in which a great bitterness was developed against the young actress, who was ambitious to rival Wallack, Burton, and Marshall as a manager."[11] Though a large crowd gathered outside of Laura Keene's Varieties on 24 December, the doors never opened because someone had slashed the major new scenery for *Prince Charming*. Keene first blamed her own indisposition for the delay in opening, rather than publicly admit the attack. But after rumors began to circulate, Keene sensed she could benefit by showing herself to be an innocent victim and printed an advertisement offering a reward for the apprehension of the vandal. Though the perpetrator was never discovered, nor links to any other manager positively established, the incident did result in a windfall of public sympathy for Keene. The *New York Times* urged the public to let Keene have a fair trial, writing, "She has talent, tact and youth on her side. If she have but discretion she must succeed, even if people do break into her theatre and destroy valuable scenery with their pen knives."[12] Still determined to carry on with her plans, Keene announced a familiar comedy, Boucicault's *Old Heads and Young Hearts*, which was hastily rehearsed to open the theatre on 27 December. Overwrought from the effort to launch her management despite the demonstrated ill will of a portion of the community, she fainted while attempting to deliver an opening night address, but did manage to make it through the comedy. Of course, it is entirely possible that Keene staged the faint, which suited her woman-under-duress persona.

For *Old Heads and Young Hearts* and many of the early productions at Laura Keene's Varieties, the actors received good notices, but the scenery and costumes were criticized for shabbiness, a problem Keene labored to overcome. Focusing on details of design, she developed an ability to create pleasing and spectacular stage pictures. Joseph Jefferson, who acted for Keene, noted that even in times of financial difficulty, "she displayed great taste and judgement in making cheap articles look like expensive ones, and both in her stage setting and costumes exhibited the most skillful and effective economy."[13] Keene certainly possessed a practical ingenuity for achieving stage illusions. Kate Reignolds, an actress in the company, recalled that when costumes were not ready at the last minute for a production of *Much Ado About Nothing*, Keene directed the sewing of garments on the actors and painted the trim on with black paint. Reminding the actors not to sit or brush each others' costumes, she then hurried off to dress herself.[14] Despite personal differences with Keene, Jefferson considered her an industrious and talented manager, writing, "If she could have afforded it, no expense would have been spared in the production of her plays; but theatrical matters were at a low ebb during the early part of her career, and the memorable panic of 1857 was almost fatal to her."[15] Of course, when there was money available Keene spent lavishly, and her theatre gained a reputation for its magnificent scenery.

Even in her first season as a theatre manager in New York, Keene exercised the strict control over all aspects of production that would be typical of her career. Besides acting most of the leading roles, she selected and trained the other actors, molding them into an efficient ensemble, rather than hiring stars. Selecting all the plays to be produced, she edited, adapted, and mended them to suit her needs. She designed scenery and supervised its construction and painting, as well as overseeing the design and construction of costumes and properties. During rehearsals Keene directed the stage business of all the actors, while during performances she was in complete control behind the scenes, with her authoritative manner earning her the secret nickname of "the Duchess" among company members. In addition, Keene handled all the theatre's publicity, the most extensive in its day, writing the advertising copy and press releases. Her business manager, John Lutz, wrote contracts, ran the box office, and, most importantly, guarded the money, but he had little artistic input and no authority backstage. A competent and popular leading actress, rather than a star performer, Keene truly distinguished herself through her efforts as a manager. A reviewer for the *Spirit of the Times* observed, "There are actresses of greater power and of greater fame, but none of greater—I may say none of equal—genius and taste in the mechanical work of the profession."[16]

During her first season at the Varieties, Keene presented several plays in which she had performed in California and introduced plays by Palgrave Simpson and Tom Taylor, two English dramatists she would rely on heavily during the following years. An afterpiece called *Novelty*, in which Keene appeared in the role of the Directress, a theatre manager eager to find some novelty to please the audience, was first presented on 22 February 1856. This quest for novelty, serving as an excuse to offer a compilation of both well-known and newly invented scenes and to create a number of scenic effects, was played fifty-seven times and reintroduced the next year under the title *Variety*. A more prophetic play and title can hardly be imagined, as Keene eventually became financially dependent on extravaganzas, usually containing only a sketchy hint of plot and no literary merit. Luckily, she managed to attract enough of an audience to her varied offerings during the first season to allow her to keep the theatre in operation. Fashionable audiences, including large numbers of women, had been drawn to her house mostly on the strength of the acting of both comedies, such as Knowles's *The Love Chase* and Taylor and Reade's *The King's Rival*, and melodramas, such as *The Marble Heart*. Near the end of her first season it seemed Keene had accomplished the difficult task of establishing her theatre and could begin to plan for a second season. In a book published in 1856, O. A. Roorbach, Jr., wrote:

> For the past three months, Miss Keene's work has been what may be called "up-hill," from the extreme exertion it has demanded from her. Identifying herself with an establishment which the ignorance and inefficiency of previous lessees had deteriorated almost to the last degree—assailed unmercifully, as well, because she, a woman and a stranger, had presumed to take upon herself the responsibilities of management—we rejoice to say, that she is now, so far as we can judge, on the direct road to fortune.[17]

Even more certain that Keene had proven her staying power was the *New York Herald*, which on 18 May 1856 reported that:

> The fair manageress of this splendid place of recreation has definitely put at rest all doubts that may have been entertained as to the establishment of an up town theatre upon a permanent and profitable basis. Talent, industry, enterprise and liberality have achieved the great aim of Miss Keene, and the popularity of the Varieties has become what the world calls a "fixed fact."[18]

After demonstrating her ability to compete as a manager, Keene was surprised by the loss of the lease to her theatre, and suddenly the prospect of continuing for another season seemed unlikely. Odell wrote, "The brave lady had fought an up-hill fight, and won her public. The managers were against her, perhaps on the principle that so long kept votes from women. And when victory seemed assured, Miss Keene lost the theatre on a technical quibble."[19] Keene had leased the theatre for one year at $400 per week from owner James

LaFarge with the option to renew the lease for four years from September by giving notice on 1 May, but it seems she was behind in rent and did not attempt to give notice until she was paid up in the middle of May. According to Keene, when she gave verbal notice to LaFarge he promised her the theatre and assured her that no further written notice was necessary, but by early June reports were circulating that Burton was to have the Metropolitan. Attempting to maintain her claim to the theatre, Keene sent letters to the papers to correct "unjust impressions with respect to Mr. LaFarge" and herself writing:

> I have invested many thousand dollars, and all I possess in the world, in his building; and all the profits of my arduous exertions through the past season are visible in the improvements, scenery, and decorations. Were I to surrender my rights, therefore, I should leave the house with nothing but my will and energy.

> I do not contemplate taking any such step, particularly as I have had no intimation from Mr. LaFarge that any of my rights are in jeopardy. On the contrary, having performed all the covenants of my lease, I do not believe Mr. LaFarge would be a party to any act tending to deprive me of my hard earned property. I am assured of this still further by the fact that he gave me his heartiest congratulations on my informing him that I would hold the establishment for the whole term of the several terms at which it was at my option, under the lease, to retain the house. He gave me, also, his word as a gentleman that he would do all in his power to promote my future success, together with the present of one week's rent as an earnest of his sympathy and co-operation; and he will not, I am assured, yield one tithe of his honor.[20]

Whether Keene had been deceived by LaFarge or was bluffing about her innocent belief in his assurances, she had not followed the letter of the law, and LaFarge was able to sell the building to Burton, who also took a lease on the ground, forcing her out. The feud continued in the press half the summer, with the *Spirit of the Times*, which usually supported Keene's managerial efforts, admitting that as

> the result of the expenditure of her time, energy, great and unquestionable talents, has been the very reverse of what she anticipated and desired...we feel more inclined to congratulate Miss Keene on her release from this splendid but harassing burden, than to deplore the cessation of her noble, earnest, but unsuccessful struggle, for the pecuniary prosperity which should have rewarded her efforts.[21]

Keene, however, was not willing to leave, and it took a court order to have her company removed from the theatre. In turn, Keene brought a suit against LaFarge which was not dropped until after his death in 1858, and until 1860 she continued to bill herself as lessee of the Metropolitan.

Appealing to the public to help her find another theatre, Keene received generous contributions which enabled her to have a new one built by the prominent theatre architect John Trimble. Laura Keene's New Theatre, also known simply as Laura Keene's Theatre, was located at 624 Broadway and built at a cost of $50,000 to 60,000, plus another $13,000 to buy out leases and rent the land.[22] The *New York Herald* anticipated,

> There will be a spirited competition among the Broadway theatres next fall. Burton will have a strong company at the Metropolitan, and the Broadway will make some important additions to its force of last season. Mr. Wallack will not be last in the race, and Miss Keene will have the *éclat* of a new house erected under circumstances calculated to call out the strongest sympathies on the part of the public.[23]

However, even with the construction of a new theatre guaranteed, Keene resented being cheated out of her lease, writing to her English play agent, Lacy:

> Mr. Burton has succeeded in taking my theatre from me. But they have built me another which will be far more elegant therefore his villainy will not have the effect he desired, which was to crush me. His accusation was that ''he was always the head of the drama here, before my advent as a manager, and cost what it would he would continue so,'' and so although I had a five years lease of the Metropolitan he induced my landlord to sell him the property. It was nothing more or less than a conspiracy. He is a bad man.[24]

In fact, Burton did not profit by moving into the Metropolitan, finding himself out of business within two years. On the other hand, large crowds were drawn to early performances at Laura Keene's New Theatre simply to admire the magnificent white and gold interior of the 2,500-seat auditorium after the *New York Herald* proclaimed, ''No such gorgeous a hall can be found in our city.''[25]

As the new theatre was not completed until mid-November, Keene took her company on a short tour to Washington and Baltimore, before opening her New York season on 18 November 1856 with *As You Like It*. She made an opening night curtain speech recounting the unfair loss of her old establishment, thanking her generous supporters, and praising the architect. Although the papers remarked that it was in poor taste to air grudges in this manner, Keene was adeptly converting difficult circumstances into public sympathy for her management. Her second start as a manager met with less opposition than her first. The *Spirit of the Times* wrote:

> We confess something of a *penchant* for "petticoat government" in theatrical matters; and when that government possesses all the energy and discrimination manifested by the most efficient male *Empresario*, combined with those subtle elegancies felt more than seen, which feminine taste alone can dictate, the charm becomes greater, and we unhesitatingly pronounce in favor of a lady manageress to rule the destinies of our amusements.[26]

Keene was clearly gaining respect as a manager, if she could cause a reviewer to stop and consider that a woman might possess qualities that would make her inherently superior to a man in that position. But whatever her accomplishments as a manager, Keene's gender continued to be a point of interest with the press.

During the next seven years Keene managed a commercially successful theatre with a wide range of offerings. Though she herself was especially suited to old comedy roles, she chose not to rely heavily on these pieces in order to avoid frequent direct competition with Wallack's. Instead, Keene developed a unique attraction at her house, the scenically elaborate spectacle piece, which was often a hodgepodge of stock material and topical allusions, lacking in literary value but attracting audiences with an abundance of pretty women and expensive stage effects. These entertainments were clearly assembled on the something-for-everybody principle, as demonstrated by a series of one-line ads run by Keene to excite interest in an early spectacle piece, *Young Bacchus; or, Spirits and Water*, including:

> Military Men—Did you see the Evolutions of "The Bacchus Guard" in the new burlesque at Laura Keene's Theatre last night? If not go to-night.

> Did you hear Tom Johnstone's new and screaming song in Young Bacchus last night?

> Temperance Folks—Go and hear Laura Keene lecture on the subject in the new burlesque of Bacchus to-night.[27]

Another type of play regularly produced by Keene were melodramas, such as *Judith of Geneva* and *The Sea of Ice*, which focused on the trials of sympathetic heroines. While not eliciting male critical approval, these plays drew large numbers of women, an audience Keene catered to with regular matinee performances, something of a novelty at the time. One of the most popular pieces produced by Keene, *The Sea of Ice*, an adaptation of a French melodrama, combined the attractions of a suffering but eventually triumphant heroine with thrilling scenic effects. First presented from 3 November to 19 December 1857 and later revived when a money maker was required, *The Sea of Ice* involved such complicated stage machinery (to create the effect of a shipwreck in an icy sea) that no afterpiece was given when it was performed. As Keene became increasingly proficient at presenting scenic wonders, even the critics praised her ability, though expressing their wishes that audiences could be attracted for good drama rather than beautiful stage pictures.[28]

In planning her seasons Keene made a real effort to include plays by American writers. The opening night playbill for the 1857–58 season announced that "while selecting such pieces as have been stamped with transatlantic success, the management will also endeavor to present such American plays, of modern and historical nature, as will tend to the establishment of a truly American drama."[29] In declaring such a policy just five years after coming to America, Keene sensed in the growing nationalism a demand for American plays. And though she continued to depend on English plays, she chose not to promote the superiority of her imported drama, but enthusiastically to embrace American plays when she could find them. Among her more successful American pieces were E. G. P. Wilkins's local comedy *Young New York* and two plays set at the time of the Revolutionary War, *Love in '76* by Oliver Bell Bunce and a version of *Blanche of the Brandywine* by Joseph Jefferson and James G. Burnett, who was Keene's stage manager.[30] Another American comedy, Charles T. P. Ware's *Splendid Misery*, which depended on topical humor concerning the financial panic of 1857, failed miserably. It apparently struck too near the worries of the audience to be amusing. Keene's own adaptation of an Irish novel, *The Macarthy; or, the Peep of Day*, was one of the adaptations, translations, and short afterpieces that added to the number of American authors—never an overwhelming percentage—presented during her management.[31]

Several plays produced by Keene had notably long runs and were, therefore, closely identified by the public with her management. One such remarkably successful play was Tom Taylor's *Our American Cousin*, which Keene had placed on the bills 18 October 1859 with some reluctance, to buy extra preparation time for an elaborate production of *A Midsummer Night's Dream*. Not only was she not especially enthusiastic about the play, her company offered further resistance to its production, challenging her authority to select plays and assign roles. Though Jefferson was pleased with the Yankee title role, William Blake refused the part he was assigned, and Charles Couldock and E. A. Sothern accepted theirs with great reluctance.[32] Sothern, who finally agreed to take the role of the eccentric Lord Dundreary on the condition that he could build up the part, added silly business such as skipping and hopping about the stage to show his contempt for the character, but, ironically, his efforts delighted audiences and he became famous in the role, eventually touring in his own adaptation of the play entitled *Dundreary*.[33]

Keene's difficulty in securing the cooperation of her popular leading actors demonstrates a difficulty shared by all managers. The problem could have been easily exacerbated whenever actors were uncomfortable assuming a subordinate role to a woman. Only through stern discipline of the company was Keene able to maintain the power and privileges of management. Company member Kate Reignolds recalled feeling that she was the group's scapegoat for a time, taking more than her share of the criticism. However, Reignolds also reported that Keene believed that the discipline had been useful, helping the young actress to mature and develop character.[34]

Keene intended her discipline for the entire company, as indicated by the "Rules and Regulations of Laura Keene's Varieties under the Management of Laura Keene":

1. Gentlemen, at the time of rehearsal or performance, are not to wear their hats in the Green Room or talk vociferously. The Green Room is a place appropriated for the quiet and regular meeting of the company, who are to be called thence, and thence only, by the call boy, to attend on the Stage. The Manageress is not to be applied to in that place, on any matter of business, or with any personal complaint. For a breach of any part of this article, fifty cents will be forfeited.

2. The call for all rehearsals will be put up by the Prompter between the play and farce, or earlier, on evenings of performance. No pleas will be received, that the call was not seen, in order to avoid the penalties of Article Fifth.

3. Any member of the Company unable from the effects of stimulants to perform, or to appear at rehearsal, shall forfeit a week's salary, and be liable to be discharged.

4. For making the stage wait, fifty cents.

5. After due notice, all rehearsals must be attended. The Green Room clock or the Prompter's watch is to regulate time; ten minutes will be allowed, (the first call only), for difference of clocks; forfeit, twenty-five cents for every scene—the whole rehearsal at the same rate, or four dollars at the option of the Manageress.

6. A Performer rehearsing from a book or part at the last rehearsal of a new piece, and after proper time given for study, forfeits one dollar.

7. A Performer introducing his own language or improper jests not in the author, or swearing in his part, shall forfeit one dollar.

8. Any person talking aloud behind the scenes to the interruption of the performance, to forfeit fifty cents.

9. Every Performer concerned in the first act of a play to be in the Green Room dressed for performance, at the time of beginning as expressed in the bills, or to forfeit five dollars. The Performers in the second act to be ready when the first finishes. In like manner with every other act. Those of the play, to be ready to begin the farce, or to forfeit one dollar. When a change of dress is necessary, ten minutes will be allowed.

10. Every performer's costume to be decided on by the Manageress, and a Performer who makes any alteration in dresses without the consent of the Manageress, or refuses to wear them, shall forfeit for each offence or omission, one dollar.

11. If the Prompter shall be guilty of any neglect in his office, or omit to forfeit where penalties are incurred, by non-observance of the Rules and Regulations of the Theatre, he shall forfeit for each offence or omission, one dollar.

12. For refusing, on a sudden change of play or farce, to represent a character performed by the same person during the season, a week's salary shall be forfeited.

13. A Performer refusing a part allotted him by the Manageress, forfeits a week's salary or may be discharged.

14. No Prompter, Performer, or Musician, will be permitted to copy any manuscript or music belonging to the Theatre, without permission from the Manageress, under the penalty of fifty dollars.

15. Any Performer singing songs not advertised in the bills of the day, omitting any, or introducing them, not in the part allowed, without first having consent of the Manageress, forfeits a night's salary.

16. A Performer restoring what is cut out by the Manageress, will forfeit one dollar.

17. A Performer absenting himself from the Theatre of an evening

when concerned in the business of the stage, will forfeit a week's salary, or be held liable to be discharged at the option of the Manageress.

18. In all cases of sickness, the Manageress reserves the right of payment or stoppage of salary during the absence of the sick persons.

19. No person permitted, on any account, to address the audience, but with the consent of the Manageress. Any violation of this article will subject the party to forfeiture of a week's salary, or a discharge, at the option of the Manageress.

20. Any new rules which may be found necessary shall be considered as part of these Rules and Regulations, after it is publicly made known in the Green Room.

* Ladies and Gentlemen bringing servants, must on no account permit them behind the scenes.

* Ladies and Gentlemen are requested not to bring children behind the scenes, unless actually required in the business.

* It is particularly requested that every Lady and Gentleman will report to the Prompter their respective places of residence.

* Ladies and Gentlemen prevented attending the rehearsal by indisposition, will please give notice to the Prompter BEFORE the hour of beginning.

* No stranger, or person not connected with the Theatre, will be admitted behind the scenes, without the written permission of the Manageress.[35]

Keene's rules and system of fines resembles the notorious list of rules that later appeared at Augustin Daly's theatre, though not extending to personal conduct.

Keene's authority was challenged by Joseph Jefferson who, rapidly growing in popularity, especially during the run of *Our American Cousin*, engaged her in a power struggle by using his new level of celebrity to make the demands of a star. After angering Keene by announcing his intention to leave her company in the fall, Jefferson insisted that his position entitled him to the role of Bottom in her long-delayed production of *A Midsummer Night's Dream*. Keene, who had planned to cast the long-idle William Blake as Bottom and Jefferson as Puck, acceded to Jefferson's demand. Unable to use the enormous Blake as Puck, she stepped into the role herself. As it turned out, Jefferson was not a satisfactory Bottom, so he agreed to abandon the role to Blake on the condition that he be allowed to leave on a starring tour of *Our American Cousin*, returning half of the profits to Keene.

This was not quite the end of Keene's trouble with Jefferson, for in the summer of 1860 he leased her theatre to present a short season with Mrs. John Wood, prompting speculation in the *Spirit of the Times* that if Jefferson were successful, he would continue to hold the lease on a permanent basis, allowing Keene to retire from management but to appear frequently as a star.[36] This report was untrue, as Keene certainly would not have agreed to work for Jefferson, given their growing antagonism.[37] It is unlikely that the *Spirit* simply meant to suggest that, all things being equal, anyone would prefer to make a comfortable living as a performer without the burdens of management, for Keene's abilities and reputation were greater as a manager than as an actress. Rather, the implication was that a woman, even one as successfully established as Keene was by this time, would prefer not to maintain the responsibilities of management if a capable man were available for the job. Ironically, when Keene finally gave up her New York theatre in 1863, the management was assumed not by Joseph Jefferson, but by his overlooked partner, Mrs. John Wood.

Managing to stay in firm control of her company despite some unhappiness over the assignment of roles, Keene mounted *Our American Cousin* and found herself with a surprise hit that ran for 140 consecutive performances on its initial presentation. That the play was first produced at Laura Keene's Theatre was a fortuitous event—Taylor had originally written it for Yankee actor Joshua Silsbee while he was working in London. The complicated history of ownership of the play and possession of the script ultimately led to law suits, for which Keene, as a busy manager, scarcely had time. Taylor had sold the play to Ben Webster, manager of the Adelphi Theatre, who planned to produce it with Silsbee in the Yankee role of Asa Trenchard. Webster, however, began to think that the fad for such plays was over and decided not to produce another one. Taylor agreed to take back *Our American Cousin* and provide Webster with a different play. Webster apparently did not return all existing copies of *Our American Cousin*, giving one to Silsbee in reparation. Silsbee later began rehearsals for a production in California, but died before he gave any performances. Learning of Silsbee's death, Taylor dug out his copy of the script and, through an agent, Bancroft Davis, sent it to Wallack. Lester Wallack said that he had no Yankee actors in his company, but suggested that the play might be suitable for Jefferson, and so the script was sent to Keene. She bought it for $1,000, at the recommendation of her business manager, Lutz. If the production of *Our American Cousin* was largely due to chance, baffled critics seemed to think the incredible success of the play was an accident. A critic for the *Spirit of the Times* later wrote:

Miss Laura Keene, with a perverseness which can only be accounted
for on the grounds of sex and profession, has the most provoking way
of always setting at naught the prognostications and wise auguries of
the critics, as well as her own speculative anticipations, failing where
success seems certain and gaining triumph from experiments that bode
little but disaster. Look back at *Our American Cousin*, tried almost
as a desperate chance, when first-class pieces, cast much better than
they ever had been before, under her management, wouldn't pay
expenses. Miss Keene herself never expected it would go, and the
critics, to a man, pooh-poohed the idea of it running through the
week. Yet it brought her crowded houses nearly all the season.[38]

While Keene had her own reservations about the play, she produced it with her
usual care and was able to draw on the comic talents of her company. Yet the
fact that she was rewarded with commercial success, despite ignoring the
advice of male critics, was seen by those critics as an example of her
inexplicable good fortune, not in any way due to her efforts to attract and
entertain a large audience.

For whatever reason, *Our American Cousin* was such a hit at Laura
Keene's Theatre that many other companies wanted to share in its popularity
and profits. Julia Daly appeared as *Our Female American Cousin*, "the
Bowery had *Our English Cousin*, Barnum reaped a harvest with *Our Irish
Cousin*, and Wood's Museum had *Our African Cousin*!"[39] There were also
many unauthorized presentations of *Our American Cousin*, including one
produced at the Arch Street Theatre in Philadelphia by William Wheatley and
John Sleeper Clarke in November 1858, using a script they purchased from
Silsbee's widow. Wheatley and Clarke also purchased instructions on the stage
business and changes in dialogue made in the Keene production from Joseph
Jefferson. Keene sued to have the production stopped, and with Tom Taylor's
support won the case. The judge decided that Wheatley and Clarke did not
possess the script legitimately and that Jefferson, as an employee of Keene,
was not entitled to sell his characterization of Asa Trenchard as developed at
her theatre.[40]

Many other productions used copies of the script pieced together from the
memory of repeat viewers of Keene's production and from the notes of discreet
paid stenographers. Keene secured an injunction against one which A. H.
Purdy opened at the National Theatre in New York City on 16 February 1859.
In many cases, such as one against E. L. Davenport at the Howard Athenaeum
in Boston during February of 1859, the producer was required only to post
bond and continued to make money during the ensuing court battle. Many
frustrating side issues in the various cases clouded the central issue of the
ownership of production rights. Moses Kimball, who produced *Our American
Cousin* at the Boston Museum in February 1859, insisted that Keene could not
bring suit against him because she was a married woman, an issue Wheatley

and Clarke also attempted to introduce into their case. The new copyright agreement offered no clear protection to a play once it was publicly performed, resulting in many interpretations of ownership. One argument against Keene asserted that she could not stop pirated productions because she had not given a written notice to her audience forbidding them to memorize the script and produce it elsewhere. Keene defended her right to the script not just on the grounds that she had purchased it from Taylor, but also on the basis of the many additions she and her company had made. E. A. Sothern was able to defend successfully his exclusive rights to his version of the play because of his own improvements on the original script. Keene continued court cases against unauthorized productions of *Our American Cousin* for ten years until a final judgment was reached against her. The court decided that she had failed to protect her exclusive right to the play because she had not brought suit against every pirated production.[41]

Another fairly long run of a play first produced at Laura Keene's Theatre was Dion Boucicault's *The Colleen Bawn*, which held the boards for thirty-eight performances to finish Keene's 1859–60 season. Boucicault and his wife, actress Agnes Robertson, had made a timely defection from the Winter Garden, giving a much needed boost to a slow season at Keene's. His version of *The Heart of Mid-Lothian*, also known as *Jeannie Deans*, opened at Keene's on 9 January 1860. In desperate need of his strong new play, Keene had relinquished her usual control over her productions, allowing Boucicault to direct the stage business and Robertson to assume the title role, foiling press predictions of violent quarrels between the two leading actresses. The press responded by praising Keene's performance in the role of Effie Deans as much as or more than Robertson's, and the play had a prosperous fifty-four-night run. Keene encouraged Boucicault to provide her with more material, but his next effort, *Vanity Fair; or, Vain of Their Vices*, was a relative failure. Urged to compose a new piece quickly, Boucicault turned to an Irish play he had begun for Mr. and Mrs. Barney Williams, based on Gerald Griffin's novel *The Collegians*, which he developed into *The Colleen Bawn*. Boucicault sent the first act and some illustrative engravings to Keene so that she could begin work while he finished writing, and the team had *The Colleen Bawn* on the stage just seventeen days after the opening of *Vanity Fair*. Audiences enjoyed Robertson as the Colleen Bawn and the redheaded Keene as the Colleen Ruahn and also appreciated the scenery, especially the sensational scene in which Myles dives into a lake, created with the assistance of twenty boys waving blue gauze.

The longest running piece ever produced by Keene was, appropriately enough, a scenically spectacular extravaganza, *The Seven Sisters*, brought out on 26 November 1860. Adapted by Thomas B. DeWalden from an old German sketch called *The Seven Daughters of Satan*, it represented a calculated gamble on Keene's part to get her theatre through difficult financial times by spending enormous sums to create the elaborate scenic illusions that were her specialty as a manager. She brought over scenic artist and machinist James

Roberts from London's Covent Garden and hired pretty, singing actresses and numerous ballet girls. Determined to achieve unrivaled scenic splendor, Keene even spent $2,000 on plate glass to create the effect of a reflecting pool in the final stage picture. Keene's biographer, John Creahan, wrote that ''the *Seven Sisters* was produced in magnificent style, its final scene, by Roberts, being the first of the grand transformation scenes which have since been made so popular by *The Black Crook*, *The White Faun* and plays of a similar character.''[42] Indeed, Keene presented her almost incomprehensible amusement featuring scenic wonders and pretty ''short petticoated ladies''[43] six years before *The Black Crook* was created. Loosely constructed around the activities of mortal and immortal characters traveling about the lower regions and New York City, the plot of *The Seven Sisters* allowed for the inclusion of ballet girls executing a Zouave drill, the characters Dundreary and Asa Trenchard from *Our American Cousin*, and specialty acts by featured performers, such as a shadow dance and a series of protean changes. Though the plot lacked cohesion, the staging and spectacle were worth the price of admission for most audience members. Even the reviewers did not really seem to mind the lack of substance or even a coherent plot, at least not during the early weeks, when *The Seven Sisters* was billed as a holiday attraction. Holiday, Saturday, and Sunday matinees were added to cater to the crowds, which, undoubtedly surpassing even Keene's expectations, kept coming even after the holiday season.

The revue-type format allowed Keene to work new material into *The Seven Sisters* continually and to make changes in the cast. For example, three new scenes were added to introduce Ben G. Rogers in February of 1861, while T. B. Johnstone's part was written out of the show after his death. This flexibility aided a feature of *The Seven Sisters* that became more important as the run lengthened: the inclusion of patriotic and political spectacle and incorporation of the changing war news. On 11 February 1861 the play acquired a subtitle, *Columbia and Her Thirty-four Daughters*, the afterpiece was dropped, and a feature called ''Uncle Sam's Magic Lantern,'' a series of tableaux on the great tragedy of Secession, was added. The *Spirit of the Times* reported, ''As events occur in the last preparation for the coming bloody struggle, the management here take directly hold of the incidents and incorporate them, either in language, or by picture, into that incongruous something or nothing, the 'Seven Sisters.' Each night the visitor is likely to hear or see something new.''[44] While the show gathered energy from current events, its primary appeal was the distraction it provided, giving playgoers a dose of ''fun, frolic and patriotism.''[45]

Keene kept the profitable *Seven Sisters* on the boards through the summer of 1861, attracting tourist and some repeat business. She herself dropped out of the production on 17 June to take a vacation, but the run continued until 10 August 1861, when it finally ended after 253 consecutive performances. By this time the critics had lost whatever initial delight they had felt for the production. Odell reflected:

> The long run of that piece might well have caused Miss Keene
> financial happiness, but it also should have caused her to reflect
> seriously on the declension in art indicated by her lapse from the
> earlier high standards of her management. Yet any one, I presume,
> would be glad to keep a theatre open on any terms during the dread
> early months of the Civil War. Art can die from inanition.[46]

Keene possessed a real talent as a director, which allowed her to turn
theatrical fluff into a popular success on the strength of staging and production
elements. Unfortunately, she mistakenly believed that this ability would allow
her to rely indefinitely on substandard dramatic fare. Keene's theatre was
never able to recover fully from its loss of artistic credibility brought on by
The Seven Sisters. Most damaging was the length of the run, during which
Keene offered no more substantial fare. She might have been forgiven a
limited run of holiday nonsense to generate income, but during the long life of
The Seven Sisters Keene lost her regular audience.

Provoking a certain amount of curiosity about her 1861–62 season simply
by refusing to reveal her plans, Keene finally announced that her first
production would be *The Seven Sons*, readily identifiable as a reworking of *The
Seven Sisters*. The *Spirit of the Times* observed:

> Having tried, convicted, condemned and executed the Legitimate, old-
> fashioned Drama, the Public is rejoicing at this moment in sensation
> shows. Laura Keene, with a woman's tact, began with just what
> Public Taste wanted—glorious scenery, pretty women, patriotic
> nonsense, hits at the war, &c., and she is having her reward in
> crowded houses.[47]

Keene's commercial success, grudgingly acknowledged by the critics as in
the statement above, was explained away as a woman manager's overeagerness
to please an ignorant public. Once again with *The Seven Sons*, though dramatic
substance was lacking, Keene's careful attention to production elements with
no expense spared succeeded in drawing an audience. "If such scenery could
be 'married to immortal verse'," suggested the *Spirit of the Times*, "instead
of the wishy-washy stuff it now redeems, what a splendid treat it would
make."[48] After one hundred performances *The Seven Sons* was removed
from the bills on 24 December 1861, and the rest of the season was filled with
revivals and other novelties, such as *Reason and Folly; or, Life in Paris*, which
featured Keene in nine roles, most of them male.

In the fall of 1862 Keene made one last attempt to live up to the former
expectations for her management and rival Wallack's again by presenting
standard favorites in repertory. Anticipating the new season, the *New York*

Herald wrote:

> We believe it is Miss Keene's intention to discard, at least for the
> present, the sensation drama, and to produce the good old standard
> comedies, which, after all, possess the most permanent elements of
> success and popularity. With the material furnished by the company
> she has gathered about her, she may safely venture the experiment,
> and rest confident that her efforts will be properly appreciated by the
> public.[49]

Despite critical support for the season, public appreciation did not
materialize, for in selling long runs of single productions Keene had lost the
patrons who had formerly visited her theatre on a regular basis. By this time
the public could be lured into Keene's theatre only with a special attraction,
and after a two-month attempt at the old standard repertory, Keene conceded
the experiment and gave the public a new extravaganza. Called *Blondette; or,
the Naughty Prince and the Pretty Peasant*, the piece, as expected, had
wonderful scenery. The *New York Sunday Times* described it as "the most
superb spectacle ever produced in this city. In 'The Seven Sisters' and kindred
pieces, Miss Keene far surpassed all other managers previous to her time in
'scenic splendours' but in 'Blondette' she has surpassed herself."[50] *Blondette*
opened on 25 November 1862, and Keene left it enjoying a profitable run on
5 January 1863, when she embarked on a starring tour of Boston, Philadelphia,
and Washington with a few of her stronger company members. Mrs. John
Wood stepped in as acting manager of the theatre, and when attendance at
Blondette began to fall off, she performed in a number of pieces, supported by
Keene's remaining company members. Keene enjoyed the short tour, which
gave her the variety of changing plays nightly and the opportunity to perform
some of her better roles, and she decided it was time to give up her New York
theatre. Before starting on a longer tour, she returned to New York and from
16 March through 8 May 1863 produced a series of farewell performances and
benefits for her company members. Mrs. Wood then took the lease to the
theatre and reopened it as the Olympic, receiving a much more encouraging
welcome than had been given Keene eight years earlier.[51]

During the next ten years Keene played acting engagements around the
country, often touring with her own company, and briefly managed the
Chestnut Street Theatre, Philadelphia, in 1869. In sharp contrast to her years
in New York, Keene met with only slight to moderate success on the road,
partly due to poor health and advancing age, but also because she was not
really a star performer. Her usual repertoire included leading roles, but not
starring vehicles. Some of her parts, such as Florence Trenchard in *Our
American Cousin*, provided no special challenges and could have been handled
by almost any actress. The later years make clear that Keene's popularity was
based as much upon her managerial skill as it was on her acting ability. Not

a star managing a company in order to spotlight her own acting and to claim a larger share of the profits, Keene was concerned with coordinating all the elements of production. With her careful attention to detail and liberal investment in her productions, Laura Keene's Theatre led New York in scenic splendour and marvelous illusions.

Keene entered the managerial profession at a difficult time, but her theatre survived the financial panic of 1857, which forced rivals Marshall and Burton out of business, and the uneasy early days of the Civil War. Introducing frequent matinees and encouraging the long run of carefully and expensively produced single plays, Keene was in the vanguard of her profession. Her theatre was a commercial success for a respectable eight years, even though, as the first woman to manage a large first-class house in New York City, she had to overcome specific opposition to her management, as well as more subtle and pervasive attitudes against women in business. Leaving no room to doubt her ability to hold a leadership position, she managed her company with strict discipline. As she proved herself a capable manager, opposition faded, and though women theatre managers continued to encounter critics, Laura Keene was frequently cited as an example that women really could be successful managers.

NOTES

1. Keene claimed to have requested and received permission to be absent from Wallack's on the night in question. After the event she wrote to local papers defending her absence on account of family matters and gained a good deal of public sympathy. J. H. Stoddart, later a member of Keene's theatre company, recalled in *Recollections of a Player* (New York: The Century Company, 1902) that a number of patrons had petitioned Wallack to reinstate Keene (it would not have been unusual to punish this first offense with a stiff fine), but he refused. It seems likely that Wallack had gained some knowledge of Keene's intentions to leave his theatre, and so felt no obligation to her.

2. Joseph N. Ireland, *Records of the New York Stage from 1750 to 1860* (New York, 1866–67; reprint, New York: Burt Franklin, 1968), 2:611.

3. *Spirit of the Times*, 15 December 1855, 528, and 21 June 1856, 228, and George C. D. Odell, *Annals of the New York Stage* (New York: Columbia University Press, 1927–41; New York: AMS Press, 1970), 6:431.

4. Besides large ads with detailed information about the program to be presented, Keene sometimes used a technique (also used in many newspapers to sell other items such as medicines) of repeating words or phrases to form large blocks of print, designs, or oversized words down the page. See, for example, the *New York Herald*, 30 January or 1 March 1859. Keene also used the technique of quoting positive notices in her ads; see the *New York Herald*, 16 October 1862, 7.

5. *Spirit of the Times*, 15 December 1855, 528.

6. Odell, 6:450.

7. Ibid., 451.

8. *New York Evening Express*, 22 December 1855, 4.

9. *New York Times*, 24 December 1855, 4, and *New York Tribune*, 24 December 1855, 2. Dorothy Jean Taylor identified this tactic of Keene's in "Laura Keene in America, 1852–73" (Ph.D. diss., Tulane University, 1966), 4.

10. For example, in her end-of-season farewell address Keene again touched on the theme of her ill treatment due to gender. She said, "It has been positively stated that I am a woman. That I have no right to a managerial chair...and that unless I can meet the attack as a man, I had best own myself conquered. I plead guilty to the charge of being a woman, and hope I have brought no discredit on my sex by my appearance as a manageress." The critic recording the address, however, stongly disagreed with all of Keene's suggestions that she had been attacked for being a woman. *New York Times*, 23 June 1856, 8.

11. "Laura Keene the Actress," *New York Times*, 20 June 1886, 10.

12. *New York Times*, 27 December 1855, 4.

13. Joseph Jefferson, *The Autobiography of Joseph Jefferson* (London: T. Fisher Unwin, 1890), 187.

14. Catherine Mary Reignolds-Winslow, *Yesterday with Actors* (Boston: Cupples and Company, 1887), 71–2.

15. Jefferson, 187.

16. *Spirit of the Times*, 21 March 1863, 48.

17. O. A. Roorbach, Jr., *Actors As They Are: A Series of Sketches of the Most Eminent Performers Now on the Stage* (New York, 1856), 43.

18. *New York Herald*, 18 May 1856, 1.

19. Odell, 6:455.

20. *Spirit of the Times*, 14 June 1856, 216.

21. Ibid., 21 June 1856, 228.

22. The *New York Herald*, 21 July 1856, 1, estimated the building cost at $50,000 plus $6,000 for ground rent, while the *Spirit of the Times*, 22 November 1856, 492, reported that the cost was $60,000 exclusive of ground rent. Taylor, 114, estimates that the cost of the theatre was $60,000 to $75,000, based on details of a dispute over the title to it reported in the *New York Tribune*, 2 May 1859, 7.

23. *New York Herald*, 21 July 1856, 1.

24. Laura Keene, letter to Lacy, 31 August 1856, in the Billy Rose Theatre Collection, New York Public Library at Lincoln Center.

25. *New York Herald*, 16 November 1856, 1.

26. *Spirit of the Times*, 15 November 1856, 184.

27. *New York Herald*, 6 January 1857, 3 (ads also ran on other dates).

28. For example, a clipping labeled *Spirit of the Times*, 28 March 1858,

in the Locke Collection, envelope 888, the New York Public Library at Lincoln Center, expressed the wish that Keene would select good dramas to produce, rather than catering to the popular taste with melodramas and spectacle. However, the reviewer acknowledged that economic necessity influenced her decisions.

29. Playbill, 31 August 1857, quoted by Odell, 7:29.

30. Jefferson, 189.

31. Early in 1862, Mrs. D. P. Bowers was also presenting a version of *The Macarthy*, hers written by Edmund Falconer, and she announced her exclusive right to the work, inciting the papers to accuse Keene of plagiarism. Public sympathy was moved in Keene's favor when a critic, making charges against her without having seen her production, described incidents in the plot that did not occur onstage.

32. Lester Wallack, *Memories of Fifty Years* (New York: Charles Scribner's Sons, 1889), 161.

33. T. Edgar Pemberton, *A Memoir of Edward Askew Sothern* (London: Richard Bentley and Son, 1889), 20-21, and Jefferson, 197.

34. Reignolds-Winslow, 67-71.

35. "Rules and Regulations of Laura Keene's Varieties under the Management of Laura Keene," Laura Keene papers, Manuscript Collection, Library of Congress.

36. *Spirit of the Times*, 14 April 1860, 96.

37. Jefferson himself wrote in his autobiography that Keene found him difficult to manage as his popularity grew (p. 198). They apparently had several arguments as Keene attempted to assert her authority and maintain a highly disciplined company. Their mutual animosity was also noted in the press. See W. Stuart, "Sketches of Actors No. XV: Joseph Jefferson," *Spirit of the Times*, 3 May 1863, 134.

38. *Spirit of the Times*, 8 October 1859, 80.

39. Odell, 7:130.

40. "Case No. 7644, Keene v. Wheatley et al.," in *The Federal Cases: Circuit and District Courts of the United States* (St. Paul: West Publishing Company, 1895), 14:180-208. Interestingly, on 1 January 1859, before this decision, the *Spirit of the Times* had suggested that Jefferson should copyright his additions to the play in order to protect Keene's right to the production seen in her theatre.

41. Keene's efforts to protect her rights to *Our American Cousin* are discussed in Taylor and in Mona Rebecca Brooks, "The Development of American Theatre Management Practices between 1830 and 1896" (Ph.D. diss., Texas Tech University, 1981).

42. John Creahan, *The Life of Laura Keene* (Philadelphia: Rogers Publishing Company, 1987), 23.

43. *Spirit of the Times*, 29 December 1860, 272.

44. Ibid., 11 May 1861, 160.

45. Ibid., 4 May 1861, 144.

46. Odell, 7:384.

47. *Spirit of the Times*, 26 October 1861, 128.

48. Ibid., 12 October 1861, 96.

49. *New York Herald*, 16 October 1862, quoted in Creahan, 69.

50. Quoted by Odell, 7:471.

51. For example, the reviewer for the *Spirit of the Times*, 17 October 1863, 112, began a long review of Mrs. Wood's opening night with, ''Behold a new theater! The wand of Prospero was not more magical in its effects than the hammers and saws and et-ceteras which have wrought this wonderful change. Laura Keene's Theater is defunct, and the new Olympic has risen like a Phoenix from its ashes.''

4

Mrs. John Drew and Other Women Theatre Managers in Philadelphia

Philadelphia had several women theatre managers over the years including those previously discussed: Anne Brunton Merry, early in the nineteenth century, as well as Mary Elizabeth Maywood and Charlotte Cushman, in the early 1840s. Though losing ground to New York, Philadelphia was still an active theatrical city in the second half of the century, when Mrs. D. P. Bowers, Mrs. M. A. Garrettson, Mrs. John Drew, and Laura Keene managed theatres there. These later women managers in Philadelphia assumed larger responsibilities than their predecessors. Merry inherited a share in the management of a theatre when her husband died, and Maywood and Cushman, promoted somewhat prematurely, lacked the necessary authority among their peers. All three enjoyed only limited power in their managements. Mrs. John Drew, by contrast, was a commanding presence with wide respect in the community, admiration and obedience from her employees, and long-term support from her theatre stockholders during her fifteen years as manager of a stock company and thirty-one years as lessee of the Arch Street Theatre. In addition to the remarkable career of Drew, the managements of Bowers, Garrettson, and Keene demonstrate the range of experiences encountered by women in the Philadelphia theatre.

MRS. D. P. (ELIZABETH) BOWERS

In many ways Mrs. D. P. Bowers's managerial career was similar to the early struggles of Laura Keene in New York. Like Keene, Bowers faced malicious anonymous opposition, to which she responded by assuming the public persona of victimized woman. Bowers, however, was made truly distraught by the attacks, and she was not in firm control behind the scenes. She was unable to capitalize on public sympathy to make her management a success. Nevertheless, she was able to help push the door to theatre management a bit farther open, to the benefit of Mrs. John Drew.

Born in Connecticut in 1830 Elizabeth Crocker, later Mrs. Bowers, was financially dependent on her older brother John, an actor, from the time her father died when she was five years old. At age fifteen she made her debut at the Park Theatre, New York, where John was playing, and moved to the Walnut Street Theatre, Philadelphia, with him for the next season. On 4 March 1847 she married Philadelphia actor David P. Bowers and spent the next ten seasons acting with him in various stock companies there and in Baltimore. During this period Elizabeth Bowers began to develop into a leading actress, demonstrating her ability in the tragic and darkly melodramatic roles in which she would become well known. The couple spent the 1856–57 season at the Arch Street Theatre, where Elizabeth Bowers received a benefit on 5 June. Following the benefit David Bowers died suddenly of heart failure, and Elizabeth Bowers became a widow with three small children to support. Able to afford only a brief period of mourning, Elizabeth Bowers reappeared at the Arch Street in August 1857. A few months later she ventured into management.[1]

Elizabeth Bowers assumed the lease to the Walnut Street Theatre when it was given up by E. A. Marshall, who moved to the Academy of Music. Given the financial panic which had occurred in the fall, Bowers did not select an ideal time to open a theatre, but, starting her season on 19 December 1857, a week after Marshall left, she was at least able to take advantage of increased holiday theatre patronage. During the short interval before her opening the only improvements to the theatre building Bowers had time to make were a thorough cleaning and the addition of new wider seats in the orchestra for the easier accommodation of ladies' crinolines.[2] The decision to open without delay turned out to be sound, as Bowers, a popular and respected actress in Philadelphia, had no trouble attracting a large share of the holiday business to her theatre. Unfortunately, though well-known as an actress, Bowers lacked managerial experience, and did not even have trusted, knowledgeable advisers in the business. Consequently, she relied on a staff primarily retained from the previous management, including treasurer James Hutchinson. Bowers did not involve herself too closely in the day-to-day financial operations, a decision she ultimately had reason to regret. Besides staff members, she employed many of the actors left from Marshall's company, soon adding her younger sister and her husband, Mr. and Mrs. F. B. Conway; her niece, Viola Crocker; and Mr. and Mrs. John Drew.[3] Peter Richings, who had previously worked as stage manager for Mary Elizabeth Maywood, became her stage manager.

Opening her management on 19 December 1857 with Boucicault's *London Assurance* and a series of national tableaux entitled *Washington*, Bowers addressed the audience before the program began. Expressing her amazement at the role she had assumed, she said, "To-night the actress is not seen—she gives place to the new and more impressive character in which I now stand before you—the character of a Manager! The word almost takes my breath away.''[4]   She went on to raise the question of how such a tiny, delicate creature as herself could take on such a burden, but then promised to fight like the leader of an army, saying:

> I find myself in the position of Atlas (rather a little lass, for an *Atlas*, you'll say) with a miniature world of responsibility resting upon *these shoulders*! Heretofore, as a *Tragedienne*, it has been my constant study how to *die*; but henceforth, as a *Manager*, it must be my study how to *live*! However, in this last and most difficult of studies, I shall not be alone, not unassisted. With my little Army, now entrenched behind this curtain, I feel as confident and as valiant as Queen Semiramis.[5]

Bowers went on to promise to present the best new plays by native dramatists, in addition to old favorites, though critics later complained that she disappointed them in this claim, often presenting plays that were ''too venerable and dull any longer to give satisfaction.''[6] However, for her first season, which lasted through 15 May 1858, Bowers regularly drew a good house with pieces such as Charles Selby's *The Marble Heart*, Tom Taylor's *Still Waters Run Deep*, an adaptation of Charles Reade's *White Lies*, and *Esmeralda; or, The Deformed of Notre Dame*.

The local papers were at first full of friendly advice for the new manager. The *Press* warned Bowers that she was not likely to get favorable notices while her ''underlings'' behaved rudely to newspaper reporters, apparently because they did not print the ''puffs'' sent by the Walnut ''Treasury.''[7] The paper wished Bowers well but said that she needed better advice, with the implication that she was not closely supervising her own box office and front-of-house staff. Another paper, the *Sunday Dispatch*, suggested that Bowers also needed to keep a closer eye on her performers, even the most talented, such as John Drew. The paper advised, ''We would hint to Mr. Drew that it is a duty which he owes to his reputation, as well as to the theatre of which a lady is manageress, to have a little regard to decency.''[8] Drew had a tendency to insert double entendres and ''blackguard stories'' which insulted the ladies, and the paper further asserted that ''Mrs. Bowers should endeavor to render her stage pure...as much due to her own character as a woman as to the respectable audiences whom she desires to patronize her.''[9] These comments suggest that Bowers did not exert strict control over her company and staff.

At the end of the season Bowers took most of her company to New York and played a three-week engagement at Laura Keene's Theatre, while Keene's company played at the Walnut Street. The New York trip was only a slight success, and the *Spirit of the Times* found that only Bowers herself compared favorably to Keene and her company. Returning to Philadelphia, Bowers took a benefit performance on 18 June and then closed her theatre for remodeling. The improvements included new cushioned seats for the entire house, tiers of boxes rebuilt for better sight lines, new decorated curtains, and an elaborate repainting. Stockholders paid for the renovation of the theatre, renamed Mrs. Bowers' New Walnut Street Theatre, and passed along the costs in the form of a large rent increase.[10]

In addition to higher rent, Bowers faced other difficulties as she started her second season at the Walnut Street Theatre. While the theatre had been redecorated, the scenery was comprised mostly of the same old stock flats, and the lack of scenic novelty or splendor must have stood out in disappointing contrast to the new murals and fresh white and gold paint of the house. Nor was Bowers able to offer much in the way of new drama, despite having acquired a house dramatist, William Cowell, the husband of company member Anna Cruise. The difficulty of providing attractive bills was compounded by the fact that Bowers's acting strength in tragic roles led her to produce rather heavy fare. The local audiences might be coaxed into sitting through multiple acts of a tragedy if it meant seeing a touring star perform his or her specialty, but it was almost impossible to get that audience into the theatre on a regular basis to see Bowers, who did not yet have a national reputation, especially since her support in serious plays was not strong. Though she had been able to hire a few good actors, her company lacked depth; therefore, when she lost the John Drews before the second season, it was quite a blow. She was, however, able to add the Frank Drews and the E. N. Thayers, local favorites, but the company, though larger than the previous year, was not strong enough to continue to draw an audience to see old plays with shabby scenery. Finally, Bowers turned to visiting stars, but this policy backfired. In addition to costing more money, it quickly drove away her best actors, even the Conways, whose opportunities were diminished by the presence of the stars.

Increased financial pressure on her management led Bowers in November 1858 to request the theatre's books for a close inspection. Not only did she discover that it was in worse financial shape than she had imagined, but she provoked the wrath of one of her own staff members. According to a letter sent to the local paper by a friend, the culprit "assailed" her with "scurrilous, libelous and slanderous anonymous letters, which have been written, sometimes as many as six in a day."[11] James Hutchinson, who had been replaced by William Arnold as treasurer early in the season, was suspected of having some part in this campaign against Bowers and felt obligated to make a statement in the press, though his guilt or innocence was never determined. The attacks increased Bowers' sense of victimization, her understandable paranoia leading her into fights with local critics, whom she also thought were trying to force her out of management because their reviews were no longer as encouraging. Bowers was anxious about her secret enemy and fearful that she would begin to suspect disloyalty among even innocent staff and company members. These worries, along with the precarious financial position of the theatre, led her to end her management on 22 January 1859. The reviewer for the *Spirit of the Times* shared her view that she was a victim, writing, "every body will take advantage of a widow,'' but this bit of sympathy was not enough to save her management.[12]

Discouraged at her failure, Bowers published a signed advertisement in the local paper, that provided a rare public statement of the frustrations which must have been shared by many of the women who attempted careers in theatre management. After thanking the public and her professional associates, she offered a warning:

> But if any sister-artist cherishes aspirations similar to those that tempted me, I bequeath to her a brief summary of what, judging by my own experience, she may fairly anticipate as the fruit of her endeavors. She will find herself, at the termination of her adventure, with health impaired by toil and care. She will discover that the artist who both acts and manages is the hardest working and worst paid member of the whole company. The pretenses of friendship, she will find to be but the masks of selfishness. If she thwarts the sinister purposes of designing people, she will become the site of every malignant shaft. The anonymous letter-writer and covert slanderer, from their cowardly obscurity, will assail her with insults which she is powerless to resent. Calumnies, as despicable as their origin is low, will creep around her fair fame, to sting and wound, if they cannot destroy. Her domestic peace will be invaded, and her enjoyment of life poisoned by evil artifices and revengeful spite. And if she has at least the courage and strength to break through the coils that are crushing out all her faith in human character, and all the vitality of her nature, she will find herself valuing, with an estimate before unknown, the comfort, peace and security that lie in paths less pretentious and prominent.[13]

These words, written as Bowers was suffering the failure of her management amid anonymous hostility, provide a particularly sharp critique of the worries that could plague any manager. Fortunately, this cautionary note did not prevent other women, some with temperaments more suited to the pressures of the work, from fulfilling their ambitions to enter management. Bowers's own sister, Sarah Conway, would successfully manage two theatres in Brooklyn for a total of eleven years, a run ended only by her death.

The unhappy demise of her management at the Walnut Street was not quite the end of Bowers's managerial career in Philadelphia. After receiving a complimentary benefit at the Academy of Music on 4 February 1859, she decided to rent that building and present a short season in March, in an attempt to restore her good name before leaving the city to make a starring tour. She noted:

I was unwilling to depart from this city with poison left in the ears of my friends, and threats ringing in my own, and, therefore assumed, for a very limited period, the Management of the Academy of Music to secure an opportunity of vindicating my own professional renown, and of testing the great social question, if there is any security for character under the guardianship of law, or the monopoly of public opinion.[14]

This experiment in management lasted only two weeks, 13–26 March, but it was still not failure enough to crush completely Bowers's ambitions to manage a theatre, for in September 1859, after the stockholders spent $3,000 to $4,000 on renovation, Bowers again assumed management of the Academy of Music with plans to "inaugurate a thorough reformation of the drama."[15] This venture did not last beyond the end of September, as the reformation of the drama began with a play reportedly written by Bowers, *The Black Agate*, which prompted at least one critic to recommend that she not try writing any more plays.[16]   On her next program she angered the critics by presenting a piece called *Isidora of Sylvania* as a new work, then, when faced with negative criticism, revealing that the play was really a version of Barry Cornwall's *Mirandola*. She suggested that, since the original was acted by Macready at Covent Garden in 1821, the critics should have recognized it.   Not surprisingly, the critics retained little sympathy for this manager, and she left town under a cloud.

Despite her disappointment as a manager, Bowers went on to an amazingly successful career as an actress, touring the country in her favorite dramatic roles, such as Lady Audley, Queen Elizabeth, and Lady Macbeth, for the next thirty-five years. She was married briefly to a Dr. Brown, and after his death married James McCollum, her touring partner for many years. In later days, before her death in 1895, Bowers was able to look back at her early venture into management without bitterness, recalling, "I had a stock company of my own in that city. Philadelphia is very dear to me."[17]

MRS. M. A. GARRETTSON

Following Bowers as manager of the Walnut Street Theatre was another woman, Mrs. M. A. Garrettson. Becoming the proprietor after her husband's death in 1858, Garrettson decided, perhaps due to the example of Bowers, that she would like to be a manager as well.   The transition from Bowers's management to Garrettson's was anything but smooth, with Will Sidney, a *Spirit of the Times* correspondent, reporting, "A civil war is going on at the 'Walnut' between the old lessee, Mrs. D. P. Bowers, and Mrs. Garrettson, the special partner, the whole assisted by Dr. Brown, C. H. Pannell, James H. Hutchinson, and F. B. Conway. Why should the *public* be worried with the private affairs of any company?''[18] The public, in fact, was not given all the details of the dispute, but it seems likely that Bowers owed money, and that Garrettson, as theatre owner and new manager, did not wish to release her from her obligations. Though Garrettson took charge of the theatre immediately after Bowers's departure and began booking in star performers, no lessee of the Walnut was named in the advertisements for the rest of the 1858–59 season. Perhaps Garrettson wanted to begin management on a trial basis, or she may simply have wanted to announce her management properly at the beginning of a new season, as her name first appears at the start of the next season, on 21 August 1859.

Not an actress herself, Garrettson was not concerned with showcasing her own talents and concentrated her efforts on engaging stars. She included in her first full season E. L. Davenport, Maggie Mitchell, Barry Sullivan, Miss J. M. Davenport, Emma Waller, J. B. Roberts, Mr. and Mrs. Barney Williams, and Matilda Heron Stoepal. Unlike Bowers, whose management had failed after she turned to stars, Garrettson's success was built upon the stars she was able to present at the Walnut. Operating the theatre as a businesswoman, she invested her money in star engagements and made star salaries a budget priority. During her management stars were not brought in as an expensive gamble to save a faltering season. When Garrettson wanted to save money, she would scrimp not on stars, but on scenery, cleaning and redecorating the auditorium, or supporting players. Surprisingly, Garrettson was able to round up a strong stock company during the early years of her management. At various times she employed Sam Hemple, Peter Richings, Cornelia Jefferson, Edwin Adams, Fanny Wallack, G. Vining Bowers, Anna Cowell, John McCullough, L. R. Shewall, and James Herne. The most remarkable feature of her management was that she made a lot of money on the venture and did not lose it before she retired from the business. Garrettson left a house and over $75,000 when she died in July 1903, years after her retirement.[19] Relying on stars to attract crowds, she eventually received extensive criticism for scrimping on scenery, costumes, and even lighting, while the quality of her supporting company declined, but under her management the Walnut Street was indisputably a commercial success.

A severe criticism of the Walnut Street from a Philadelphia paper called the *City Item* was reprinted on 4 October 1862 in New York's *Spirit of the Times* as part of a correspondent's report.

We are sorry to see that no steps have been taken to make the nuisances of the Third Tier less disagreeable to the audience; the matter is becoming so notorious that ladies cannot, with propriety attend, and we wonder that the fair Lessee can sit in her box, night after night, knowing that these shameless scenes are enacted in the theater, without some effort to remove them. We are sorry to be compelled, also, to allude to the stench which arises from the long neglected boxes and parquette of this theater. It is true that the building is old, but that is no reason why it should be dirty. Because peanuts are good, it does not follow that the shells should lie about the floor, nor because large numbers of the audience chew, is there any reason why tobacco juice should flood the floors.[20]

The following week the *Spirit of the Times* apologized for printing the notice, claiming it "would not have been suffered in this paper, if it had not escaped observation before it was printed," and assuring its readers that "we hold Mrs. Garrettson to be as respectable a lady as any in the profession."[21] Yet, despite the paper's denial, there may have been some truth to the report, for other papers also observed a decline in the condition of the house. The "nuisances of the Third Tier" is a reference to prostitution, an evil long associated with the theatre.[22] It would not have been surprising for Garrettson to try to ignore such activity rather than eradicate it, for the experience of other managers demonstrated that clearing the third tier could mean quite a loss of revenue for a theatre, and she was clearly more interested in profits than a high reputation for her house. Though the status of the theatre was no longer first class by 1862, it was still a profitable venture, and the *Spirit of the Times* reported that "despite all the attractions elsewhere, [she] manages to hold her own and maintain the popularity of her establishment, as a star theater."[23] Garrettson finally abandoned management in early 1865, when she sold the Walnut Street Theatre to Edwin Booth and John Sleeper Clarke.

MRS. JOHN (LOUISA LANE) DREW

While Garrettson was still managing the Walnut Street Theatre, another woman, Louisa Lane Drew, began her managerial career at the Arch Street Theatre. Assuming the management in 1861 and continuing for more than thirty years, with an active stock company for the first fifteen, Drew had the longest career of any American woman theatre manager during the nineteenth century and was one of the most outstanding managers of the period. Unlike most other women managers, she was invited to the job, warmly welcomed, and loyally supported. Early in 1861, after William Wheatley and John Sleeper Clarke announced their departure, she was asked to become manager of the Arch by its board of directors. Reportedly, Adam Everly, son of the board's president, suggested Drew for the job, pointing out her "experience, ability, good taste, and judgement" and referring to Laura Keene's success in New York to counter any hesitation to leasing the theatre to a woman.[24] After writing for the consent of her husband, who was on tour in England, Drew accepted the position.

Drew certainly had a great deal of relevant experience for someone who had not actually managed a theatre at that time. Starting her career as an infant carried onstage by her mother in England in 1820, Drew, then known as Louisa Lane, found almost continual employment from her first American appearance, which took place on 27 September 1827 at the Walnut Street as the Duke of York to Junius Brutus Booth's Richard III. For several years Louisa Lane performed as a child star, often in protean roles such as all the Mowbrays in *The Four Mowbrays*, before making the transition to adult roles in her early teens.[25] She toured extensively as an adult under the names Mrs. Henry Hunt, Mrs. George Mossop, and finally Mrs. John Drew, gaining a national reputation as a versatile, popular actress and working for a large assortment of managers. Further opportunity for her to observe a manager at work was provided by her third husband, John Drew, who comanaged the Arch Street Theatre with William Wheatley from 1853 to 1855 and managed the National Theatre in Philadelphia during the summer of 1857. The latter venture, however, provided an example of the hazards of the business, as the Drews had to sell their home in order to clear the debts from the failed enterprise.[26] "There was probably not one who possessed a better all-around equipment for her profession," recalled the *New York Dramatic Mirror*, noting that Drew was quite an experienced actress when she became manager, and "in addition, her judgement as to the practical affairs of life was excellent."[27]

An advantage possessed by Drew in her efforts at managerial success was her air of authority, a quality not enjoyed by all the women who attempted management. A commanding presence was a boon to any manager trying to draw the best possible performance or technical assistance from a large company and staff, but such a presence was especially useful to a woman manager in an age when women employers were a novelty. *Green Book Magazine* later described her as "born for leadership, with the power to govern and direct rarely seen in one of her sex."[28] Drew had a regal bearing which led her employees, like Laura Keene's, to call her "the Duchess" in secret. "Some women descend to bullying to maintain their authority—not so Mrs. Drew," recalled Clara Morris, a visiting star at the Arch Street Theatre. "Her armor was a certain chill austerity of manner, her weapon a sharp sarcasm, while her strength lay in her self-control, her self-respect."[29] Drew exercised her authority by maintaining strict discipline over her company, closely supervising their behavior throughout four hours of daily rehearsal and during each performance. If the work done in her theatre did not measure up to her standards, she had a quietly theatrical method to signal her dissatisfaction. Company member A. Frank Stull recalled:

> Mrs. Drew had a way of putting up for a long time with things that she felt should be remedied; but, little by little, as her patience ebbed, her silence would become more pronounced, like the lull before the storm; then, some day, upon arriving at the theatre, she would walk into the box office and don a certain red shawl which she kept in reserve as one of the most impressive pieces of stage property in the

house. It fittingly reflected her mood. So long as that shawl was in evidence, all the people of the Arch, from stage carpenter to leading man, realized that perfection in the performance of duty was the smallest return they could give for their salaries.[30]

Calling her mother "a woman of extraordinary force of character," Georgina Drew Barrymore noted:

The management of a stock company in those days was no easy task, and without a firm and judicious hand at the helm shipwreck was a sure and certain eventuality. Now, my mother not only possesses wide experience, but she has had the faculty of maintaining a discipline which never slackened for a moment. Her talents as an actress gained for her the respect and veneration of the company, and with respect was mingled a dash of wholesome fear, which even the boldest was not ashamed to acknowledge, for she was always just and never tyrannical.[31]

Beyond her stern fairness, Drew's authority was based on her vast knowledge of the stage. Describing her many talents, T. Allston Brown wrote that

she produced a reform in the manner of placing pieces on the stage. A great many old actors have told me that she is the best stage-director ever seen. As the principal stage carpenter of the "Arch" once said to me with pride, "Why, sir, there ain't a carpenter in the theatre whom she can't sometimes teach how to do a thing." Her glance was everywhere. Her judgement and taste were carried into every department. Her administrative powers are remarkable.[32]

Drew's commanding air was not merely a theatrically assumed attitude, but a visible confidence, based on relevant experience and wide-ranging ability. Such certainty of purpose and calm exercise of power inspired the trust and support of her company, staff, and stockholders, resulting in a success built on her self-assurance.

As Drew's actors learned to meet her exacting standards, they improved in their craft, and Drew earned a reputation as a trainer of actors. The careful attention she paid to training actors was mostly due to necessity, for the supply of actors was low when Drew began her management, and throughout the years she lost many of her better players to New York managers.[33] Still, Drew saw that it was in her interest as a manager to make the best of the actors she employed, rather than to try to shine more brightly as a star by surrounding herself with barely adequate support. The actors, who practiced their art in daily ten A.M. to two P.M. rehearsals conducted by her, were expected to be punctual, serious in their work, and quick in learning lines. Drew herself, with a remarkable memory developed while studying lengthy protean roles as a child, came to rehearsals not only letter-perfect in her own roles, but for standard pieces knowing all the other parts as well. As a result of the regular, no-nonsense rehearsals, first performances of any given piece at the Arch Street Theatre were extremely well played by the standards of the day, with few missed cues or fumbled lines.[34]

This thorough preparation, based on extensive knowledge of traditions of the stage, helped Drew earn a good reputation for her theatre, though, unlike Keene, she was not known as an innovator. In fact, she resisted change in some matters of theatrical production. Most notably, she resisted the change from stock to combination companies, maintaining her stock company through 1876 (and organizing pick-up companies when needed through 1879), despite the appearance of more traveling stars on her bills. Regular matinee performances, popularized by Keene, were added on Saturdays in 1874 by Drew, but only reluctantly, for they reduced the available rehearsal time. The scenery she used at the Arch was in the traditional wing and shutter style, though new scenes were painted and special effects produced when required, to provide novelty and prevent criticism that the scenic elements were overlooked. In selecting a repertory Drew balanced her favorite old comedy pieces with newer melodramas and local-interest pieces, though, of course, when stars visited the Arch they played their own selections. Astutely, she developed a company that, while designedly stronger in comedy than tragedy, which Drew rarely acted in or produced, was not dependent on her presence as a star. She was careful not to wear out the popularity she had earned during many years before Philadelphia audiences. Instead, her appearances which became less frequent during her management were always a bonus that could draw a crowd.

During her years as manager of the Arch, Drew took good care of the theatre building, supervising major renovations and daily maintenance. She redecorated the house, replaced all the seats, laid a new floor, improved the ventilation system, and acquired furniture and a new drop curtain for the stage before opening her first season in 1861.[35] She also sent a clear signal that she expected to draw a respectable audience to the Arch by replacing the third tier with an amphitheatre and by removing the theatre's bar.[36] After rejuvenating the theatre, Drew insisted that it be kept remarkably clean, for the comfort of both audience and actors. "What a paradise her theatre was to the actress who wore fine costumes—such immaculate cleanliness from footlights straight to the building's walls!" recalled Clara Morris. "The floor was scrubbed to a creamy purity, everything that could possibly bear a coat of white paint had it. Cellars and darksome corners, usually reserved for the propagation of spiders and evil musty odors, responded wholesomely to the healthful effects of the whitewash brush."[37] In contrast to Garrettson's reported neglect of the Walnut, Drew's unusual attention to cleanliness and upkeep reflects a managerial style stressing personal involvement and maximum effort in all endeavors.   During the summer of 1863 she oversaw an even more extensive renovation of the Arch, including the removal of boxed tiers in favor of a more open, democratic arrangement in the newly enlarged auditorium.   With this renovation the manager's name was added to the structure's appellation on all bills, making it Mrs. John Drew's New Arch Street Theatre, and so it remained, through a subsequent remodeling in 1871, until Drew gave up the lease in 1892.

Drew's active participation in all aspects of theatrical production also extended to her theatre's financial department, where she worked closely with business manager Joseph Murphy.   Personally distributing salaries each Saturday, she was able to claim she never failed to meet her payroll, though in her first season she was forced to borrow money week after week.[38] During that season the treasurer reported at the stockholders annual meeting in early February that $3,658.51 had been spent of $3,660.75 received.[39] With only fourteen hundred seats, the Arch was a small theatre, so profits were limited, and it was not possible to make a great surplus on a hit to pay for leaner times.   Still, the Arch managed to stay afloat, and Drew continued to inspire the confidence of the stockholders, who decided to spend large sums renovating the theatre, lowered the rent during especially difficult times, and never offered the lease to anyone else.   Ultimately, Drew proved worthy of such confidence, as the value of stock in the Arch rose from $500 to over $750 a share, and then available only upon the death of a stockholder.[40]   Drew herself managed to support several dependents on her income from the theatre, and she did quite well during good years, for example, reporting $11,552 in taxable income for 1864.[41] Certainly, the total record is impressive, as Drew managed to keep the Arch in operation and profitable overall during a period of thirty-one years.

LAURA KEENE

Another management of a Philadelphia theatre by a woman during this period deserves mention, though it lasted less than a full season. Laura Keene, after several years on the road, decided to take up full-time management again at the New Chestnut Street Theatre.   Built in 1862 the New Chestnut Street suffered from shortages of material and skilled labor brought on by the Civil War and was a small, unattractive house, given over to the production of variety entertainments.[42] The theatre did have the advantage of being situated in a fashionable area; therefore, Keene remodeled the interior and attempted to convert it into an elegant, first-class house. Forming a company from actors who had toured with her, supplemented by Philadelphia actors, she presented a season beginning on 20 September 1869. It included many standards of her repertoire, such as *The Marble Heart*, *Our American Cousin*, *Masks and Faces*, and *Two Can Play at That Game*.   The most unusual feature of this management was a set of special matinees featuring plays for children, including *Bold Jack the Giant Killer* and *Little Red Riding Hood*. Unfortunately, neither the families for the matinees nor the fashionable evening audience was large enough to keep the New Chestnut Theatre in business, so by the end of March 1870 Keene abandoned her last managerial enterprise and resumed touring with a small company.[43]

Though Keene's efforts as a manager in Philadelphia were not profitable, she did not face opposition on the grounds that she was a woman, as she had during her early days in New York. This was, of course, due to the fact that Philadelphians had seen several women managers by the time she arrived on the scene. Though the earlier women managers did not have a great impact on theatrical affairs in the city, they did prepare the way for later successful managers such as Garrettson and Drew. Bowers, the one who seemed to encounter the most personal opposition to her management, is a transitional figure in the history of women managers in Philadelphia, for unlike the earlier Merry, Maywood, and Cushman, she came to management completely of her own volition and made a serious attempt to take charge of every aspect of her theatre and assume responsibility for its success. Both Garrettson and Drew were clearly in control of the operation of their theatres and demonstrated their ability to manage by their financial success—and in the case of Drew's Arch Street Theatre, with artistic success as well. With the longest managerial career of any nineteenth-century American woman, Drew provides an example of the highest achievement in theatre management, training actors and mounting popular productions in a well-regulated theatre which ran at a profit.

NOTES

1. T. Allston Brown, *History of the American Stage* (1870; reprint, New York: Burt Franklin, 1969), 45, and Kathleen Anne Morgan, "Of Stars and Standards: Actress-Managers in New York and Philadelphia, 1850–1880" (Ph.D. diss., University of Illinois, 1989), 19–20.

2. Morgan, 22–23.

3. Mari Kathleen Fielder, "[Third] Walnut Street Theatre Company," in Weldon B. Durham, ed., *American Theatre Companies, 1749–1887* (New York: Greenwood Press, 1986), 535.

4. *Philadelphia Daily News*, 21 December 1857, 3.

5. Ibid.

6. *Press* (Philadelphia), 4 September 1858, 1.

7. Ibid., 18 January 1858, 2.

8. *Sunday Dispatch* (Philadelphia), 31 January 1857, 3.

9. Ibid.

10. Fielder, 536.

11. *Sunday Dispatch* (Philadelphia), 23 January 1859, 2.

12. *Spirit of the Times*, 29 January 1859, 612.

13. *Sunday Dispatch* (Philadelphia), 23 January 1859, 2.

14. *Press* (Philadelphia), 19 March 1859, 3.

15. *Sunday Dispatch* (Philadelphia), 21 August 1859, 2.

16. Ibid., 11 September 1859, 3.

17. *Spirit of the Times*, 7 March 1874, 87. Another positive reflection on her managerial days in Philadelphia is found in the *Daily Picayune* (New Orleans), 8 April 1894, 26.

18. *Spirit of the Times*, 5 February 1859, 619.

19. Copy of will in clipping file, Free Library of Philadelphia, Theatre Collection.

20. *Spirit of the Times*, 4 October 1862, 77.

21. Ibid., 11 October 1862, 93.

22. See Claudia Johnson, *American Actress: Perspective on the Nineteenth Century* (Chicago: Nelson-Hall, 1984), 13–17, and Claudia Johnson, "That Guilty Third Tier: Prostitution in Nineteenth-Century American Theaters," in Daniel Walker Howe, ed., *Victorian America* (Philadelphia: University of Pennsylvania Press, 1976), 111–20. Johnson uses the example of Edmund Simpson, who suffered great financial losses when he attempted to clear the third tier of the Park Theatre, New York, in 1842. He ultimately gave up.

23. *Spirit of the Times*, 14 February 1863, 384.

24. *Philadelphia Evening Bulletin*, 14 September 1897, in clipping file, Harvard Theatre Collection.

25. Mrs. John Drew, *Autobiographical Sketch of Mrs. John Drew* (New York: Charles Scribner's Sons, 1899).

26. Dorothy E. Stolp, "Mrs. Drew, American Actress-Manager 1820–1897" (Ph.D. diss., Louisiana State University, 1953), 233–34.

27. *New York Dramatic Mirror*, 11 September 1897, 15.

28. *Green Book Magazine*, August 1912, 335. The piece also claimed that if Drew "were a figure in present day affairs there is little doubt that she would be a militant suffragette." I disagree with this assessment, for there were militant suffragists (the correct, nonderogatory term for American women campaigning for voting rights) in Drew's day, but her interest, talent, and energy were completely absorbed by the theatre.

29. Clara Morris, "The Dressing Room Reception Where I First Met Ellen Terry and Mrs. John Drew," *McClures* 22 (December 1903): 210.

30. A. Frank Stull, "Where Famous Actors Learned Their Art," *Lippincott's Monthly Magazine*, March 1905, 373–74.

31. *Philadelphia Public Ledger*, 2 September 1897, 3.

32. T. Allston Brown, "Mrs. John Drew," in Frederic Edward McKay and Charles E. L. Wingate, eds., *Famous American Actors of To-Day* (New York: Thomas Y. Crowell and Company, 1896), 133.

33. C. Lee Jenner, "The Duchess of Arch Street: An Overview of Mrs. John Drew's Managerial Career," *Performing Arts Resources* 13 (1988): 35.

34. Morgan, 40.

35. *Sunday Dispatch* (Philadelphia), 25 August 1861, 2.

36. Ibid., and *Philadelphia Evening Bulletin*, 14 September 1897.

37. Morris, 210.

38. Drew, 110.

39. *Inquirer* (Philadelphia), 3 February 1862, reported in Stolp and in Jenner, 32.

40. Brown, 131.

41. Income information drawn from the *Inquirer* (Philadelphia), reported in Morgan, 58.

42. Mari Kathleen Fiedler, ''[New] Chestnut Street Theatre Stock Company,'' in Durham, 213.

43. John Creahan, *The Life of Laura Keene* (Philadelphia: Rogers Publishing Company, 1897), 31–37.

5

After Keene—More Women Theatre Managers in New York City and Brooklyn

After Laura Keene established herself as manager of a first-class New York City theatre, overcoming objections that a woman could or should not attempt to realize such ambitions, several more women managers appeared on the theatrical scene in New York. Not surprisingly, since theatrical production was a high-risk business enterprise for anyone, many were unsuccessful. Still, the existence of a small but significant number of women determined to test their ambitions, leadership skills, and business sense in the theatre is worth noting during an age when women found few business opportunities or managerial positions. The existence of less successful and less well-known women managers also provides a perspective for viewing the careers of the few more familiar names among nineteenth-century women theatre managers, showing them to be not isolated aberrations, but the more prosperous representatives of a substantial presence.

One of the prominent women managers in Keene's wake was Mrs. John Wood, who assumed the management of the theatre Keene vacated. Renaming it the Olympic, she managed it profitably for three years before returning to her native England, where she continued her career as an actress and manager. Another woman who had an outstanding managerial career in the New York City area was Mrs. F. B. (Sarah) Conway, the first manager to establish a permanent stock company in Brooklyn. After Wood and Conway several other women, no longer perceived as oddities, tried their luck and ability in New York.

BELL CARR

Several women enter the record only briefly as managers, including Bell Carr, who began her management of the National Theatre in New York City on 25 June 1859. A reviewer for the *New York Herald* noted that there was only a fair house for opening night because the company members were not well-known, but predicted success for the theatre if subsequent performances met the standard set by the first night.[1] Carr, who first appeared with her company on the fourth of July, presented a varied program of mainly comedy and pantomime. She engaged Little Lola to play in several pieces, including a version of *The Old Curiosity Shop*, from 4–9 August. Fanny Herring and Miss A. Hathaway played a special engagement at the National from 22–27 August. On 27 August 1859 Carr, apparently short of cash, advertised for a managerial partner.[2] Evidently unable to attract additional investment in her scheme, she took two benefits on Saturday, 3 September 1859, to close the theatre.

WEBB SISTERS

The following spring one unfortunate theatre at 444 Broadway, between Howard and Grand streets, saw the failure of three successive managements led by women. The first was that of Ada and Emma Webb, a young acting duo, who toured extensively in the United States between 1859 and 1869. They opened the theatre as the Broadway Boudoir on 18 January 1860 and rechristened it the Webb Sisters' Theatre on 6 February.[3] The Webbs usually presented three comic pieces each night, relying most heavily on two protean vehicles: *The Four Sisters,* with Emma impersonating all four, and *Woman's Whim; or, More Changes Than One*, which featured Ada as six different characters.[4] Limited in their managerial options by a fairly small performance repertoire, the Webbs remained in business for only three more weeks. Never again attempting management, they toured together until Ada married in the summer of 1869 and Emma took to the lecture circuit.[5]

MRS. CHARLES HOWARD

The Webb sisters were followed by Mrs. Charles Howard, who on 27 February 1860 opened the theatre as Mrs. Charles Howard's Broadway Boudoir. First known professionally as Rosina Shaw, one of the singing Shaw sisters, she had married Charles Howard in 1845 and established herself as an actress in burlesque and farcical pieces. After the death of Charles Howard in 1858, Mrs. Howard married Harry Watkins but retained the stage name of her previous husband.   Watkins supported his wife's managerial enterprise, appearing in the company and serving as stage manager.   The opening production, a dramatization of Mrs. E. D. E. N. Southworth's *The Hidden Hand*, ran through 10 March. A few more pieces were tried with *The Romance of a Very Poor Young Man*, a burlesque by Charles Gaylor, dominating the bills for the rest of the season, which was terminated on 31

March.[6]   Quite possibly Mrs. Howard considered her management of the Broadway Boudoir as an extended tour stop in a city with a large theatregoing population.   On 5 May 1860 Mrs. Howard and Harry Watkins sailed to England, where they stayed until 1863.[7] Mrs. Howard continued her acting career, becoming known for the old women's parts she played until her death in 1891.[8]

MRS. JOHN (EMMA WILLIAMS) BROUGHAM

The next manager of 444 Broadway was Mrs. Brougham, first wife of actor-manager-playwright John Brougham.   Born Emma Williams, she had married Brougham in England in 1842 and came to the United States with him, divorcing him in 1852.   In 1853 she became Mrs. Robertson and retired from the stage for a time, but she retained the name Mrs. John Brougham (under which she debuted in New York on 4 October 1842 at the Park Theatre) as a stage name.   On 7 April 1860 Mrs. Brougham's Theatre, also known as Mrs. Brougham's Broadway Boudoir, opened its season of light comedy, farce, vaudeville, and burlesque at prices of fifty cents or less.   "Mrs. Brougham's Theatre is doing an excellent business, presenting light comedies well played, for a small sum," reported the *Spirit of the Times*, adding on 5 May, "Mrs. Brougham is succeeding admirably, and if she continues in her present course, her theatre will become a necessity for the New York public.   She has selected a very excellent company, and some of the prettiest girls on the stage.   Young as well as old New York like this feature."[9]   The low admissions apparently did not cover the expenses of an excellent company with pretty girls, and the season was ended abruptly on the day the positive notice appeared, 5 May 1860.   Emma Brougham ventured into management on one other occasion, leasing and remodeling the Broadway Theater, formerly the French Theater opposite Niblo's, in September 1863.   The second management lasted only two days before negative public reaction and Brougham's "serious illness" forced her out of business.[10]

MARY PROVOST

On 17 March 1862 Mary Provost reopened the old Wallack Theatre on Broadway near Broome Street as Mary Provost's Theatre.   Provost herself did not appear on opening night or during the first three weeks, instead presenting as a guest star John Wilkes Booth, in one of his two New York appearances.[11]   By the time Provost first appeared in the second week of April, there had been a fair amount of hype in the press, partly based on her appearance at the Princess Theatre in London the previous summer, asserting that she would soon be recognized as a great tragic actress.   Though Provost had been born in Brooklyn in 1835 and had debuted at the Federal Street Theatre in Boston in 1849, she had spent most of her career in California and Australia, and New York audiences were not familiar with her work. By opening a New York theatre under her own management, Provost found the opportunity to promote her own acting career, focusing attention on herself as she stepped into the role of leading lady in the country's theatrical capital. As a manager she took a big gamble, for unlike many actresses making the move into management, she did not possess the asset of a devoted local following eager to support her efforts. Although Provost did create interest in her venture, she was not able to convert it into long-term support.

After just two weeks of performing Provost fell ill and had to suspend her theatrical activities for a time, making it difficult for critics to evaluate her success. "The experiment of restoring Wallack's old theatre is not yet fully tried. It is up-hill work, and the enthusiastic lady who has undertaken the task—Miss Mary Provost—deserves warm and generous encouragement,'' wrote the critic for the *Spirit of the Times*, who also noted that Provost had a potential not yet realized during her short career as a New York actress-manager:

In consequence of ill health and inefficient support, this young lady has not come before the public in a manner to warrant extended and particular criticism, and as, for the present at least, she is not before the footlights, I shall defer comment until she has a better opportunity of proving her title to the high rank which is claimed for her. The little that I have seen inclines me to the belief that she has a great many personal and mental advantages, with real talent of no common order; and though shining with diminished lustre during her present effort, there is no doubt that under circumstances reasonably favorable, she will justify very much—perhaps all—that has been predicted.[12]

While actresses frequently developed convenient "illnesses" to allow them to depart gracefully from a stage failure, Provost seems to have had authentic health problems, widely discussed in the press during the next few years, which often caused her to delay or interrupt engagements.[13] Near the end of April 1862 Mary Provost's Theatre was briefly converted to George Fox's Olympic, Fox's management lasting only through 10 May. There followed several reports that Provost would resume her managerial efforts, and late in June she did make a short return to the theatre, now called the Olympic, but was unable to satisfy the critics who had declined to judge her harshly in April. She failed to establish herself as a manager or big-name star, though she did continue to tour in tragic and melodramatic roles for several years as her health permitted.

MRS. JOHN WOOD

In contrast to Provost, Mrs. John Wood was already a popular performer with a large following in New York when she entered the management business. A hit with New York audiences since her first appearance at Wallack's during December 1856 and January 1857 as Minnehaha in *Hi-A-Wa-Tha; or, Ardent Spirits and Laughing Waters*, a burlesque by Charles Walcot, Wood played frequent starring engagements in New York and other eastern cities between 1859 and 1862. She also had the advantage of at least limited managerial experience, having briefly managed the American Theatre in San Francisco and the Forrest Theatre in Sacramento. A further, unique advantage was the opportunity she had had as guest star and temporary manager of Laura Keene's Theatre in early 1863 to observe the theatrical business climate and to become closely acquainted with Keene's theatre. When Keene returned to New York in mid-March to play a series of farewell performances, Wood decided to secure the lease to the theatre for the next season.

Renaming Laura Keene's Theatre the Olympic Theatre, Wood also redecorated the house that had been built for Keene in 1856. In terms of technical production Wood followed Keene's example, spending generously, even lavishly at times, on costumes, scenery, and special effects. Like Keene, Wood produced several spectacle or extravaganza pieces employing beautiful stage pictures and lots of singing and dancing. Her rather eclectic offerings included adaptations of Dickens's novels and a revival of Boucicault's *The Streets of New York*, but instead of the sentimental melodramas Keene often relied on, Wood favored the short burlesques that showed her to best advantage. At the end of her first season the reviewer for the *Spirit of the Times* assessed her record as a manager: "Mrs. Wood has worked hard and done pretty well. However her cash account may stand, she has honestly earned more than any other Broadway manager, having given the public a greater number of pieces, and got them up in better style."[14]

Wood possessed a rare comic talent that in large measure accounted for her continuing popularity with audiences. Observers of her acting reported that she had tremendous energy with which she could transform a poorly written scene into an amusing one, spark the other actors onstage to give better performances, and carry every nuance of expression across the footlights and directly to the audience. Her good-natured stage persona, overflowing with comic inspiration, reportedly contained "the very element of fun" which "simply bubbled up within her."[15] Kate Reignolds recalled that Wood's acting style combined "innocent impudence and saucey effrontery, which made you catch your breath for fear of what might come—but never did."[16]

As Wood captivated audiences without fail, she tended to outshine her company members during the first weeks of her management. She soon hired a number of talented actors, including Mrs. G. H. Gilbert, James Lewis, William Davidge, James H. Stoddart, Charles Wyndham, Frank Drew, J. K.

Mortimer, John Dyott, Lotty Hough, and Eliza Newton, and developed a first-class company that could hold its own even when she herself was not performing. The popularity of both actress-manager and her company resulted in a profitable operation. The biggest hit of the 1864–65 season at the Olympic, *The Streets of New York*, demonstrates this point. It held the boards for sixteen weeks, though Wood did not appear in the spectacular revival. However, the largest single night's receipts, a sum of $1,344.70, was collected on 3 April 1865, when Wood reappeared on her stage to take a benefit as Lady Gay Spanker in *London Assurance*. [17]

Wood was still at the height of her popularity in New York when she decided to give up the lease to the Olympic and return to England. As managements were typically abandoned due to financial failure or, at least, a trend of falling receipts—and this was not the case with Wood's management—the announcement of her imminent departure was greeted by surprised disappointment from both her regular audience and professional colleagues. James H. Stoddart recalled, "I was with her during the three years of her management, and her retirement from it caused great regret, not only on the part of the public, but also to all her associates."[18] The *Spirit of the Times* asserted that "with her the very genius of fun has departed and Comedy weeps through her mask."[19]

Wood's decision to terminate her New York management seems to have been based primarily on her desire to return to her native land and, using the knowledge, experience, and capital acquired as a manager in the United States, establish herself as an actress-manager there. Though she had been born into an English theatrical family and had acted for several years in the provinces, she was known in London only by her American reputation. As if the burden of being regarded as an American was not enough, Wood chose to lease a London theatre, the St. James's, which had proven unfortunate for other managers. Tracking her activities from New York, the *Spirit of the Times* issued dire warnings: "She must surely be aware of the dangerous character of the St. James's, and we can hardly suppose that she esteems herself capable of suddenly reversing the ruinous course of a house which, even when controlled by the ablest hands in England, has brought nothing but disaster to its lessees."[20] Though still pessimistic, a month and a half later the *Spirit of the Times* conceded that "all that energy and experience can do toward reshaping the destiny of the house she has chosen will be at her command. Her task will be laborious but she is not the woman to shrink from it on that account."[21]

In fact, Wood successfully transformed the St. James's Theatre into a popular house, managing it for a total of eight years, at times subletting it to other managers while she pursued separate acting projects. Making a return visit to the United States, she joined Augustin Daly's company for most of the 1872–73 season, before leaving to resume managerial duties at the St. James's. Wood later managed a few seasons at the new Court Theatre, London, beginning in 1888. She last appeared on stage in 1905 and died in 1915.

MRS. F. B. (SARAH) CONWAY

During Wood's term at the Olympic another important woman, Mrs. F.B. (Sarah) Conway, began her managerial career in Brooklyn, which was not yet part of New York City. Born Sarah Crocker in Connecticut in 1834, she followed her brother John and sister Elizabeth (Mrs. D. P. Bowers) on the stage, debuting at the National Theater, New York, in 1849. Acting at the Broadway Theatre, she met and, by mid-May 1852, married Frederick B. Conway, an English actor almost twice her age. For the 1853–54 season he remained at the Broadway while Sarah worked as a leading juvenile at Wallack's Theatre, stepping into leading lady roles for a short time after Laura Keene's sudden departure from that institution. Sarah Conway then rejoined her husband, acting with him in various stock companies, including her sister Elizabeth Bowers's company at the Walnut Street Theatre in Philadelphia in 1858. She also had the opportunity to observe managerial tasks at close range when her husband undertook short stints as manager of Pikes Opera House, Cincinnati, and of the Metropolitan Theatre (late Burton's) in New York from 4 April through 25 June 1859. After a trip to England in 1861 the Conways toured in the United States, arriving in Brooklyn and taking the lease on the Park Theatre in April 1864.

At the time of the Conways' arrival, Brooklyn did not yet have one permanent theatre supporting a regular stock company. One large theatre, the Academy of Music, was sometimes visited by star actors, but theatrical production was not the chief focus of the house, which featured concerts and lectures. A businessman and writer, Gabriel Harrison, marshalled growing local interest in a permanent professional acting company for Brooklyn into a campaign to build a new theatre, the Park. He also became the theatre's first lessee and manager. Harrison opened the new Park Theatre, on Fulton opposite City Hall, on 14 September 1863, but soon failed. Although he quickly disbanded his acting company and instead booked in opera troupes, he was still unable to keep his lease past February 1864. The Conways, who came on the scene with professional experience and popularity as performers, encouraged local hopes that Brooklyn could support a permanent stock company.

On 2 April 1864 the Conways opened their engagement at the Park Theatre, playing Mrs. G. W. Lovell's *Ingomar, the Barbarian* and the farce *My Neighbor's Wife*, with Mrs. Conway advertised as sole directress. Anticipating the opening, the *Brooklyn Daily Eagle* wrote, "We trust our citizens will appreciate the importance of giving a helping hand to this fresh enterprise. If Mrs. Conway is successful in establishing a first class theatre here she will receive, as she will merit, the thanks of the entire community.''[22] Despite this prediction, the citizens of Brooklyn did not rush to support the venture: a heavy deluge of rain thinned the expected opening night crowd. Struggling to find an audience, Sarah Conway presented a new bill almost every night, mostly of the standard fare she and her husband were used to playing, such as *The Marble Heart*, *Peep O' Day*, *Macbeth*, *Still Waters Run Deep*, *East Lynne*, and *The Hunchback*, along with farces and an occasional sensation piece like the Civil War melodrama *The Pomp of Cudjo's Cave* and a spectacular version of the Faust legend. The company was breaking even by the time its first season ended on 23 July 1864, and though ''[Mr.] Conway thought of giving it up, Mrs. Conway, a woman of much stronger will than her husband, determined to fight it out while they could pay their way.''[23] From this point on Sarah Conway, who possessed greater business and organizational skills than Frederick Conway, was clearly in charge of operations at the theatre, which reopened on 3 September 1864 as Mrs. F. B. Conway's Park Theatre.[24]

Establishing and maintaining a successful theatre company in Brooklyn was difficult for a number of reasons. Upper-class patrons were accustomed to ferrying over to New York City to attend the theatre. While Sarah Conway's theatre offered a more conveniently located alternative, many greeted the notion of a first-class theatre in Brooklyn with skepticism. Even after they began to visit Mrs. Conway's Park Theatre, these playgoers continued to travel into New York to see new plays or favorite actors or simply for the cachet a Brooklyn theatre could never hope to possess. If a high-class audience preferring to travel across the river for their entertainment could not alone keep the Park in business, Sarah Conway reasoned that she must appeal to all classes and to a wide variety of tastes. To satisfy various types of patrons and also to encourage repeat patronage, as Brooklyn lacked New York's large supply of transient entertainment seekers, Sarah Conway changed her bill of fare frequently, despite the trend toward longer runs then seen in New York City. This practice involved additional work, especially for the actors who had to learn more roles, and a choice between greater expense and poorer quality when the pieces required extra costumes or new scenery. Another problem resulting from Brooklyn's proximity to New York was that Sarah Conway had tremendous difficulty in recruiting and keeping good actors. She usually had to select from actors who could not find suitable employment in New York. The problem seems also to have applied to musicians and stagehands, for local papers chronicle sloppy, erratic work on the part of those two groups as well.[25] Sarah Conway struggled continually to overcome the prejudice in favor of the New York stage, long held by both audiences and theatrical professionals.

Sarah Conway regularly presented the serious, standard dramas in which she and her husband liked to act, but she also made concessions to popular taste. For example, on Saturday nights she usually presented plays that appealed to ''a class which prefers a sensation above all things, which delights in blood-and-thunder villainies, with alliterative titles and which shouts 'hi hi,' and fills the house with dust in the ecstacy of its applause.''[26]   As this was also an audience expecting a large quantity of entertainment for its money, programs at the Park Theatre were often longer on Saturdays than on other nights of the week.   During the Christmas season and at other times when some novelty was desired, Sarah Conway would present a specialty piece, designed to run for longer than the usual night or two.   More money and rehearsal time could be spent on these productions, such as *The Naiad Queen*, which ran from 24 December 1864 to 20 January 1865, than was generally possible on plays that would have only an occasional showing.   One scenic sensation piece of particular significance was J. J. McCloskey's *Across the Continent*, which debuted on 28 November 1870 and went on to achieve national popularity.

Even though she produced a number of spectacle pieces, Sarah Conway was careful to strike a balance in play selection and performance style that would appeal to both the more refined leaders of the community and a mass audience.   The *Brooklyn Daily Eagle* observed,

> The manager who can so underline his plays as to bring the two classes together, and who can satisfy the one with an artistic performance, and at the same time fill the upper part of the house with an enthusiastic audience, is the man for the hour and the house. It would not be exactly in accordance with strict propriety to speak of Mrs. Conway as the 'Man of the Hour,' but we desire emphatically to record her success.[27]

Part of her success was clearly due to her ability to please popular tastes while still upholding standards appropriate for the "city of churches." When ballet girls were employed in one of Sarah Conway's productions, the local press sometimes commented on their decent attire and deportment, for example, writing that "the girls challenge comparison with the handsomest of the Crookites,'' that is, performers in the notorious leg drama *The Black Crook*. "It is such a rarity to find lady-like looking and well-behaved girls in the ballet or in the minor departments of any of our theatres, that it is a positive duty to note this feature in our only Brooklyn theatre.''[28]

Another way Sarah Conway varied her bills was by presenting visiting stars, infrequently at first, but more often in later seasons.   The visiting star engaged most regularly over the years was her sister Elizabeth Bowers, who had gained a reputation as a tragic actress.   Other stars who appeared at the Park included Charlotte Thompson, Lawrence Barrett, E. L. Davenport, John Brougham, Lucille Western, Edwin Adams, Kate Reignolds, Joseph Proctor, and Emma Maddern, although often the better stars opted to play at the larger Academy of Music.   The presence of stars freed Sarah to spend more time on managerial concerns and allowed both Conways (each normally appeared only with stars of the opposite sex) a respite from acting duties. This was important because they, especially Frederick, were increasingly ill as the years passed. The star engagements also kept local audiences from getting bored with the couple and made Sarah Conway's return to the Park after an absence seem like a special occasion. One problem with presenting star performers was that the discipline and quality of work exhibited by the supporting company tended to decline when Sarah did not appear in the program. While she was able to exert some control over her actors when they were under her eye, she lacked Mrs. John Drew's famed ability to strike fear in the hearts of actors which encouraged their best efforts even when she might not be present. Unfortunately, she also lacked Mrs. Drew's talent for training young, unknown actors to meet the requirements of her theatre; therefore, despite her much-praised acting ability, the second-rate actors she often hired out of necessity tended to remain second-rate.

Local newspaper critics, who had been quite supportive of Sarah Conway's early efforts at the Park in the hope of finally seeing a professional acting company reside in Brooklyn, became more critical after the company began to be seen as an established fact. Community expectations evidently increased, and audience members became less likely to tolerate problems, such as poor actors in secondary roles, in the interest of supporting the local company. Each season Sarah Conway stayed in business she was, therefore, under pressure to raise her theatre's production standards. Late in her career, when interviewed for the *Spirit of the Times*, she revealed just how troubled she had been by negative notices in the press, saying that the critics

> have attacked me without cause, and maligned me without foundation....I have had to contend against them for a long time. They recently united to attack me so persistently that I would retire in disgust, in order that one of their crowd might get possession of it and assume its management. But they found out their mistake, and know by this time that I am not to be driven from my position, or intimidated by their vapid threats.[29]

For the most part, however, it seems reviews accurately reflected the mixed performance of Sarah Conway's company over the years. Though the level of production was not consistently high, she was capable of producing plays that rivaled New York in quality. She frequently presented the latest dramatic hit through deals she made with New York writers and managers, such as Augustin Daly.

The acting of the Conways drew praise, and although that of other company members was often criticized, the press at least acknowledged that the regularly performing company was superior to the hastily assembled pick-up companies that supported visiting stars at the Academy of Music. The *Brooklyn Daily Eagle* reported:

The occasional dramatic entertainments at the Academy of Music are a direct penent [*sic*] to Mrs. Conway. They illustrate the advantage of a permanent theatre, and the superiority of a regular stock company over the aggregation of stray talent picked up to support stars. Accustomed to see plays well cast and carefully acted throughout, with complete appointments and appropriate scenery, at the Park, people get severely critical over the disconsolate sticks who wander over the bleak desert of the Academy stage, with its shabby scenery and destitution of properties.[30]

Overall, the press never attacked any aspect of production at the Park for very long without stopping to praise Sarah Conway's efforts. Complaining at length about the pieces she selected to please the popular taste, the critic for the *Brooklyn Daily Eagle* conceded that she

has rent and salaries to pay, herself and family to support, and not being blessed with a private fortune she must make money enough to meet all these incidental expenses or shut up the Park Theatre. Like a sensible lady, she does the best she can for her art—endeavors to please the public and to keep her head financially above water. If the theatre going public of Brooklyn will not have good plays at any price she must necessarily let them have such as they prefer to pay for, unless she is ready to take the benefit of the bankrupt act.[31]

Sarah Conway had always found the Park Theatre, built above a basement level saltwater bathing business and first floor shops, to be a bit cramped. With fewer than one thousand seats it could not hold a big enough crowd when a popular attraction was scheduled. For several seasons in a row, for example, her own year-end benefit was held at the Academy of Music in order to accommodate all who wished to attend. For this reason she collaborated with several Brooklyn business leaders to form the Brooklyn Building Corporation and build a new fifteen hundred-seat house, the Brooklyn Theatre, which she opened on 2 October 1871 with Bulwer-Lytton's *Money*. Unfortunately, the move to a new, larger theatre after seven seasons at the Park brought an unexpected decline in Sarah Conway's managerial fortunes. Once the new facility was in operation, many patrons, especially the upper class which still preferred to visit New York City theatres, expected a significant improvement in the level of performances. In fact, the quality remained little changed. Another factor was a decline in the national economy following the great Chicago fire of 1871, which may have prompted a reduction in money spent on entertainment. Repeated serious illness on the part of Frederick prevented him from acting and distracted Sarah from her managerial concerns. Finally, she had hired a large stock company of nearly fifty actors, with the result that there was little money left to hire visiting stars, to the disappointment of the public.

Sarah Conway preferred a strong stock company to a string of visiting stars because of the greater unity that could be achieved when a group played regularly together without the need of adjusting to a new star every two weeks. She also defended the old policy of casting by lines of business and was unhappy with the decline in moral decency she saw in contemporary "society plays."[32] Like Mrs. John Drew she was slow to add matinee performances, not doing so regularly until the 1870–71 season. Despite her own reluctance to alter tradition, Sarah Conway always considered her audience and adjusted accordingly. In the case of the star policy at the new Brooklyn Theatre, she eventually hired John P. Smith as business manager in 1874 and let him book numerous star engagements while she took short tours with a few of her company members. With the regular appearance of star performers the Brooklyn Theatre began to be more profitable, but the Conways were unable to enjoy the change in its fortunes. On 8 September 1874 Frederick died, followed by Sarah herself on 28 April 1875.

Despite the sometimes uneven quality of her company, Sarah Conway made a significant contribution to the American theatre as the first manager to establish a permanent company in one of the country's largest cities, Brooklyn. The first American-born woman to manage a theatre successfully over a number of years, she had a managerial career of eleven years, which was ended only by her early death at age forty-one. She was well respected within the profession, reportedly causing theatre manager Lester Wallack to remark, "If I were not Lester Wallack I would be Sarah Conway."[33]

After Sarah Conway's death, her twenty-one-year-old daughter Minnie, an actress with Augustin Daly's company, attempted to manage the Brooklyn Theatre, hoping to support herself, her sister, Lillian, age sixteen and also an actress, and her brother, Frederick, age eleven, and to maintain the family home, apartments above the theatre. Receiving a benefit at the Academy of Music on 8 May 1875, the Conway sisters then reopened the Brooklyn Theatre on 10 May with Hart Jackson's adaptation of Adolphe D'Ennery and Eugene Cormon's *The Two Orphans*, which had been playing at the theatre with Lillian as one of the orphans before their mother's death. Minnie assumed the role of the other orphan, and the piece ran through 25 May 1875, when the sisters closed it for the season, announcing their intention to resume management in the fall. Minnie Conway was soon faced with legal and financial difficulties. Sarah Conway, unable to meet the $18,000 annual rent on her new theatre the first year, had been excused from paying several thousand dollars during her management, but when Minnie made $5,000 in current rent payments, the debt forgiveness was rescinded and all the money was applied to her mother's debt by theatre owners William Kingsley and Abner Keeney. With her inheritance and benefit proceeds suddenly vanished, Minnie threatened to remove scenery, which had been purchased by her mother, from the theatre, but was legally barred from taking such action. Having no other available course of action, she resigned the lease in July in exchange for a receipt for all past rent.[34] Both sisters continued their acting careers, though neither was as successful as their parents. In later years Minnie became the mother of English actors Godfrey and Conway Tearle, while Lillian organized and toured with the Lillian Conway Opera Company in an effort to support herself and two children after separating from her husband.[35]

LUCY RUSHTON

The success of women theatre managers, such as Laura Keene, Mrs. John Wood, and Sarah Conway, encouraged other women, some with lesser gifts, to try their luck. One woman to enter the managerial field with far more ambition than talent was Lucy Rushton. An English actress, she apparently paid for the opportunity to make her American debut at Mrs. Wood's Olympic Theatre on 2 October 1865.[36] Rushton appeared in an insubstantial piece called *Lolah*, and the critic for the *Spirit of the Times* declined to pass judgment on the actress until seeing her Rosalind, *As You Like It* being next on the bills. However, he did observe that Rushton was very blond and blue-eyed with a stout, well-formed body covered by a robe which should have been more sewn up in front, suggesting that Rushton's greatest asset was her physical attractiveness.[37] Although her Rosalind was pronounced a failure and an embarassment for Mrs. Wood, Rushton acted as if she had launched her New York career with a triumph and decided to carry her success one step further by opening her own theatre.

"Miss Rushton, whose brief engagement at the Olympic was conspicuous, is transforming the Church of the Messiah into the New York Theatre, and promises to open this week," reported the *Spirit of the Times* on 23 December 1865. Funding for the venture had apparently been provided by A. T. Stewart of department store fame,[38] prompting the critic for the *Spirit of the Times* to muse,

> As the enterprise is doubtless supported by our own capital, it may not be impertinent to ask what special reason there can be for withholding similar assistance from American artists who are literally dying to figure in management? What potent charm is there in this beautiful alien blonde, to enlist that material aid and comfort for which scores of actresses vastly her superiors in excellence have sighed in vain? When this house celebrates its first anniversary we may be wiser.[39]

Lucy Rushton's New York Theatre did not survive long enough to provide an answer.

Opening on 23 December 1865 with *The School for Scandal*, Lucy Rushton's New York Theatre had been converted from a church in only sixteen days. The architectural problem of the transformation "puzzled the builder not a little, and we don't think he's got the right answer," reported the *Spirit of the Times*, "To be sure, he has run a brick and wooden portico half-way up the front, but this in no way hides the true character of the edifice, but only makes it look like a church with a petticoat on. Perhaps, however, this effect was intended in compliment to the new manager."[40]   The stage was reportedly not much larger than the former pulpit and was by far the smallest theatrical performing space in the city. Rushton assembled a rather impressive company on the tiny stage, including Charles Walcot, J. K. Mortimer, Mrs. Mark Smith, and Clara Fisher Maeder, although several players, including Walcot and Mortimer, defected as the season progressed.

After a couple weeks of old comedy, Rushton began presenting burlesques, musical and spectacular pieces, and while the theatre was not a lasting success, neither was it an immediate failure. On 17 February 1866 the *Spirit of the Times* reported, "This house has drawn a prize in the managerial lottery, by the production of a burlesque by Mr. J. Schonberg, on the Hibernian drama of *Arrah Na Pogue*, entitled *Between You and Me, and the Post*."[41] Another play by James Schonberg, Rushton's stage manager, billed as the new, spectacular burlesque *Valient Valentine*, was announced on 31 March 1866. The critic for the *Spirit of the Times* hoped it was not really being produced at great expense, as receipts even for crowded houses at the small theatre could not meet a large expense, and also expressed scepticism about grand transformations and scenic thrills being created on such a tiny stage.[42] By the next week the amazed critic called *Valient Valentine*'s final transformation "the finest ever shown in New York," and proclaimed it all the more impressive for having been accomplished in such a contracted space.[43] Still, the play must have cost more than it earned, for the following week the end of Rushton's season and term as manager were announced.

Offering a hypothesis as to why the venture failed, the critic for the *Spirit of the Times* wrote:

> Miss Rushton's mistake has been one common to women who undertake both to manage and to play; they are too fond of themselves; they must be always in the bill, and always in large type; they must have plays "doctored," or written to suit their special tastes; they must inevitably have the lion's share in the cast; and then they will not abide a handsome woman on their stage—that cannot be endured—they are, most of them, full of vanity and self-conceit, so far as their own sex is concerned. I do not charge all this upon Miss Rushton, nor upon any other in particular; indeed, there are notable exceptions—Mrs. John Wood, for instance, who does *not* insist upon playing every night, nor upon every leading part, nor is she afraid of good-looking women at her elbow. I think if Miss Rushton had depended a little less upon herself and more upon a good company,

she would have done much better—more especially since she is a stranger, and naturally cannot be very intimate with the tastes and peculiarities of our people.[44]

While the general assertion of vanity on the part of women managers seems insupportable, Conway and Drew being two important managers besides Wood who did not rely solely on their own box office appeal to keep their theatres afloat, Rushton's management was an example of a theatre built around a star-manager who was not truly of star caliber. A final benefit for Rushton was held in the theatre on 25 April 1866, and the *Spirit of the Times* urged the public to

manifest their good will to the lady by attendance. It is certain that she has made very great efforts (badly directed, to be sure) and has sacrificed a great deal of money to support her little house. The purpose was praiseworthy but the means inadequate. Now let the play-going public recognize the claims of the lady—a stranger in our city—whatever they may think of her original enterprise and its management.[45]

WORRELL SISTERS

After Lucy Rushton's departure, the New York Theatre was temporarily occupied by Sallie Hinckly, then by Mark Smith, but neither established a long-term management of the facility. Finally, the Worrell Sisters took control of the theatre, opening their management on 11 May 1867 with *Aladdin* and *Cinderella*. Sophie, Irene, and Jennie Worrell were young burlesque actresses who began their careers singing and dancing as young children under the management of their father, circus clown William Worrell. The Worrell Sisters had performed extensively in California and Australia and were familiar to New York audiences, having played at Wood's Theatre from May through July 1866 and at the Broadway Theatre in January and February of 1867. It is quite possible that the Worrell Sisters' New York Theatre was actually managed by William Worrell, who, sensing the growing interest in women managers, downplayed his own involvement. On the other hand, the young Worrells, with years of performance experience, may have been making their own managerial decisions with some advice from their father.

Playing in burlesques, which allowed them to demonstrate their singing and dancing ability, the Worrells attracted good houses for their first season, which ran until early July 1867. In the fall they sublet their theatre to Augustin Daly for the first production of his *Under the Gaslight*, beginning the middle of August 1867. The Worrells were in the audience opening night, and by October they were themselves acting in a production of *Under the Gaslight* at the Howard Athenaeum, Boston. They returned to their theatre to appear in Daly's adaptation of Henry Beecher's *Norwood*, but when that failed to draw they put on the boards their version of *Under the Gaslight*, which ran through January 1868. Daly's adaptation of Dickens's *Pickwick Papers* and Fulton's *Nobody's Daughter* were among the dramas presented by the Worrells before they returned to burlesques on 4 April 1868 with *La Belle Hélène*. Late in June a production called *The Grand Duchess* replaced *La Belle Hélène* to complete the season.

The Worrells planned to begin the 1868–69 season by once again subletting to another manager while they made a short tour to other cities. Unfortunately, they had great difficulty regaining possession of their theatre, apparently because of a loosely written sublet agreement. Dion Boucicault and Charles Reade's *Foul Play* began at the Worrells' New York Theatre on 1 August 1868, under the management of a Mr. Lloyd. The popularity of the piece sparked a rival production at the Broadway Theatre, and Lloyd secured an injunction preventing the Worrells from interfering with its run. However, after *Foul Play* ended, Lloyd retained control of the theatre and presented Charles Gaylor's *Out of the Streets* on 10 October 1868. The Worrells were reported several times to be returning shortly to their theatre, but Mrs. Scott-Siddons played an engagement at the house before they finally reappeared in mid-December. They gave up the management of the New York Theatre in March 1869, complaining that theatre owner A. T. Stewart would not maintain the building in usable condition. They published a farewell advertisement stating that "their withdrawal from the management is owing to the sincere conviction that no quality of talent could attract ladies or gentlemen into its peculiar and uninviting interior."[46]

The Worrell Sisters continued to perform for many years, both together and separately. In 1873 their name once again appeared on a theatre, this time at 585 Broadway, a house later known as Tony Pastor's Theatre. During this brief managerial stint they presented their popular pieces *Ixion* and *The Field of the Cloth of Gold*. Sophie Worrell eventually married an actor and continued her career as Mrs. George Knight, while in later years Jennie resurfaced, destitute and drunk, a pathetic creature with a happier past who sparked the interest of newspaper reporters.[47]

CATHERINE LUCETTE

Another woman, Catherine Lucette, entered the managerial ranks in Brooklyn, opening Catherine Lucette's New Theatre on 21 December 1868. Lucette was an English actress who had made her New York debut on 23 May 1859 with her husband, Captain Morton Price, at the Metropolitan Theatre. The couple soon returned to England where, according to Price, they managed theatres in London and the provinces over the years.[48] Between May and

December 1862 the *Spirit of the Times* had reported on several occasions that Lucette, or Lucette and Price together, were managing Sadler's Wells in London. Price had intended to work on a literary composition when the couple returned to New York in 1868, while Lucette wished to act. Since she was unable to secure an engagement, she went into management herself. She rented a large room, formerly used by the Republic General Committee, over the post office in Brooklyn and converted it into an eight hundred-seat theatre. Catherine Lucette's New Theatre offered light, amusing ''vaudeville'' pieces, such as the ''musical trifle'' *The Rustic Prima Donna*, presented on opening night.[49]   Captain Price appeared in his wife's productions, as did William Davidge and several little-known Brooklyn actors. The venture was not a success, and the theatre was forced to close on 6 February 1869, when the gas was shut off. However, Lucette was soon offered a position in Mrs. Conway's Park Theatre company.

LINA EDWIN

The next woman to undertake the management of a Brooklyn theatre did so as a prelude to managing one in New York City. Lina Edwin, after playing with Lydia Thompson's burlesque company at Niblo's Garden during April and May 1870, organized her own comedy and burlesque company to play during the summer season at Hooley's Opera House in Brooklyn. ''Miss Edwin has evidently had more of an eye to making a reputation than money, at the outset of her managerial career,'' reported the *Brooklyn Daily Eagle*, ''Taking advantage of the close of the New York theatres she has taken her pick of the disbanded companies and secured some of the most talented artists who have sustained the reputation of the New York stage during the past season.''[50] Among the distinguished players were Stuart Robson, Charles Vandenhoff, James Lewis, McKee Rankin, Fanny Davenport, and Marie Wilkins. The company played from 5 July until 30 July 1870, when the heat made it impossible to draw an audience. The short season received a positive critical response, which encouraged Edwin in her next project.

Edwin leased Hope Chapel, a place of amusement in New York City that was originally built as a church and had most recently been occupied by Edwin Kelly and Francis Leon. Changing the name of the hall, located at 720 Broadway below Eighth Street, from Kelly and Leon's to Lina Edwin's Theatre, she also supervised a quick renovation of her new house. On 12 September 1870 she opened with Frederick Phillips's *A Bird in the Hand Is Worth Two in the Bush* and a burlesque, *Black Ey'd Suzing; or, That Leetle Bill Which Was Taken Hup*. Presenting her company in comedies and burlesques, Edwin appeared only intermittently, concentrating instead on her managerial duties. With *Black Ey'd Suzing* and *Aladdin* on the bills on 5 November 1870 the *Spirit of the Times* reported, ''With two of the most popular burlesques, and two of the most admired burlesque actors, Messrs. Harry Beckett and Stuart Robson, with a good company generally, a very pleasing theatre, and her own stronghold upon a numerous class of admirers, Miss Lina Edwin fills her theatre nightly with excellent and highly-amused audiences.''[51] Another hit at the theatre was *Little Jack Sheppard; or, The Idle Apprentice*, which opened on 28 November 1870 and ran through December with Edwin in the title role, a popular breeches part.

Early in 1871 Edwin began to let her theatre be used by other performers and companies and ceased to maintain her own permanent company. Among the subletters of Lina Edwin's Theatre was Laura Keene, making one of her last New York appearances in Boucicault's *Hunted Down; or, The Two Lives of Mary Leigh* from 25 January to 4 March 1871. Edwin reappeared at her theatre from 9 May until 3 June 1871 in a new comedy called *Rank*. After this production her active management of the theatre seems to have ended, although the theatre continued to bear her name until August 1872. Former managers Kelly and Leon were among the performers who appeared at the house, but they did not resume the use of the name Kelly and Leon's Theatre, presumably because Lina Edwin still held the lease. The theatre was destroyed by fire in early December 1872. Lina Edwin was performing in Australia with her husband, Bland Holt, in March 1883 when she was stricken with paralysis, dying in June in Melbourne.[52]

MINNIE CUMMINGS

Minnie Cummings, much like Lucy Rushton, launched her managerial career on the strength of her ambition, rather than her talent. Having come to public attention as one of the six Juliets featured in a spectacular production of *Romeo and Juliet* at the Booth Theatre in 1877, Cummings entered management by converting the Fifth Avenue Hall, on the site of the previously destroyed Daly's Fifth Avenue Theatre, into Minnie Cummings Drawing Room Theatre. It opened on 30 December 1878 with an operatic farce, *Manhattan Beach; or, Love among the Breakers*, by Edward Mollenhaur and Charles Barnard, followed by a protean farce, *In and Out of Place*. Because Cummings did not receive capital which had been promised to her, the theatre soon was forced to close. Steele MacKaye then gained possession of the building and converted it into his Madison Square Theatre. In July 1880 Cummings starred at the Fifth Avenue Theatre in a play she had written called *Suspected*, but this venture was also less than successful. Later in life Cummings helped form the Women's Property Protection League and reportedly helped start the Actors' Fund movement when, as manager of the New Haven Opera House, she set aside a week's receipts to start a fund for indigent show folk.[53]

KATE CLAXTON

An actress who for many years traveled as head of her own acting company, Kate Claxton made several attempts to establish herself as a theatre manager. Born Catherine Cone in Somerville, New Jersey, in 1850, Claxton acted in Augustin Daly's company for two years before rising to prominence in A. M. Palmer's company at the Union Square Theatre. It was at the Union Square that she first performed the role of Louise in *The Two Orphans*, a part she would play thousands of times throughout her career. Claxton eventually purchased the rights to *The Two Orphans* from Palmer, whom she left in 1876 to begin touring with her own company. During her many years of managing a company she was frequently assisted by her brother Spencer Cone, who served as treasurer and business agent.

In the summer of 1878 Claxton secured the lease to the Lyceum Theatre in New York. Subletting it to Denman Thompson in the fall, she continued to tour during his longer-than-expected successful run in *Joshua Whitcomb*. On 2 December 1878 Claxton began her occupancy of the house, presenting the United States premiere of Charles Reade's *The Double Marriage*. This was the only piece Claxton produced before she decided to return to the road in early January 1879. She again professed the intention of establishing herself as the manager of a New York theatre, taking the lease of the Third Avenue Theatre in January 1884, but she gave up the project in February. Claxton's dependence on a limited repertory seems to have been the greatest obstacle preventing her from establishing a permanent theatre. It was simply easier for her to earn money touring in the same popular roles, especially as the blind orphan, than to establish a regular audience in New York for her new productions.

In a final major effort to control her own theatre, Claxton lost several thousand dollars during her few weeks as manager of the Park Theatre, Brooklyn, in 1899. Unfortunately, the people of Brooklyn had not forgotten the tragic Brooklyn Theatre fire of 1876 with over two hundred lives lost, which began during a performance by Claxton in *The Two Orphans*. Since that event she had been plagued by a reputation as a fire jinx in theatrical circles, but her ambition to manage a theatre in Brooklyn was judged by some to be not just unlucky but also in poor taste.[54]

Despite her own difficulties Claxton was enthusiastic about the opportunities a woman could find in the theatre. She said, "I know of no other vocation except literature in which a woman stands on a footing of absolute equality with a man. If an actress is capable of doing as good work as an actor she receives the same remuneration that he does."[55] Years of managing a touring company, along with her repeated attempts to manage a permanent theatre, suggest that Claxton saw great opportunities for women in theatre management as well as in acting. In later years she spent much of her time defending her copyright for *The Two Orphans*.

HELEN DAUVRAY

Another woman who managed a theatre in New York for a time, Helen Dauvray began her theatrical career in San Francisco as a child actor, performing for years under the name Little Nell, the California Diamond. Dauvray reportedly became wealthy thanks to a chance investment in the Comstock Mine in the Nevada territory before its great silver lode was discovered. As a young woman she went to Europe to be educated and then made her French-language debut at the Folies Dramatique in Paris on 1 September 1884.[56] For her first adult appearance in New York, Dauvray rented the Star Theatre and, beginning on 27 April 1885, presented a play called *Mona*. The expensively mounted production was not a success, though Dauvray herself was moderately well received.

In November she assumed management of the Lyceum, a theatre that had been planned by Steele MacKaye and opened on 6 April 1885 with his *Dakolar*, though a lack of funds forced him to sell it. Dauvray's business manager in the venture until his untimely death on 27 February 1886, John Rickaby, was sometimes referred to as the manager of the theatre during the early weeks of Dauvray's term. The production she chose to launch her management, Bronson Howard's *One of Our Girls*, opened on 10 November 1885 and was such a hit that it ran two hundred nights, and no other play was introduced during the first season. Daniel Frohman gained control of the Lyceum before the next year but allowed Dauvray to manage a season as a sublessee.[57]

Dauvray took *One of Our Girls* on tour in the fall of 1886 while Frohman presented a Miss Fortesque, who did not prove especially popular, at the Lyceum. Returning to the theatre on 11 December 1886, Dauvray produced *A Scrap of Paper*, Howard's new play *Met by Chance*, *Masks and Faces*, and *Walda Lamar* before she ended her management in May, surrendering the theatre to Frohman and his new stock company.[58] In 1889 Dauvray married her second husband, baseball player John Ward, and retired from the stage at his request. The early retirement led her to break a contract she had made with manager Harry Miner, which in turn prompted theatre critic Nym Crinkle to complain at length about women not keeping their business contracts. However, Nym Crinkle recalled that Dauvray had had a good business reputation and had usually acted responsibly before this incident.[59]

ROSINA VOKES

Another woman, who like Kate Claxton was primarily the manager of a traveling company, deserves mention because she regularly managed a summer season at a New York theatre. Rosina Vokes and her London Comedy Company toured extensively in the United States, making their home at Daly's

Theatre every summer from 1886 through 1893. The child of a London costumer, Vokes had first visited the United States in 1872, performing with her older siblings as part of the Vokes Family company, and returning each year through 1877. She then married Cecil Clay, a London barrister, and retired from the stage for a time.

In 1884 financial troubles prompted Vokes to form her own comedy company, with mostly amateur performers, and return to the United States, presenting programs consisting of several short skits or one-act plays. Her regular appearances at Daly's led to speculation that she would seek her own permanent theatre. Vokes responded,

> In the first place, it would necessitate my confining myself to one place, which I should not be willing to do; and in the next place, feeling that a theatre, if established, should be run on the old stock idea, that the manager should see to everything and be everywhere present, I would be compelled to give up acting, No; my wish, if carried out, would be to divide my season among some half-dozen of the leading cities.[60]

For Vokes the advantage of touring rather than managing a permanent theatre was that only a few changes of bill were needed for an entire season as long as the company kept moving from city to city. She died of consumption on 27 January 1894.

Other women about whom less information is available also managed theatres in the New York area. Rachel Denvil managed a season at the Brooklyn Opera House from June through August 1868. From 1880 to 1882 Belle Berry managed Belle Berry's Broadway Theatre in Williamsburg, now a part of Brooklyn. Fraulein Cotrelly, who later sang at English-language theatres in New York, managed the Thalia, a German theatre in New York, from at least 20 March to 27 November 1880.

By the mid-1860s the appearance of a woman theatre manager in New York City was no longer unusual enough to receive special notice. The success of Laura Keene had cleared the way for other women to enter management, and the press allowed them to go about their business without the excessive critical scrutiny that had greeted Keene. Though many of the women theatre managers had relatively undistinguished careers, their presence in the field deserves to be acknowledged as it demonstrates both their opportunities and ambitions. Some women, though now largely forgotten, such as Mrs. John Wood and Sarah Conway, had impressive careers in theatre management.

NOTES

1. *New York Herald*, 26 June 1859, 5.

2. *Spirit of the Times*, 27 August 1859, 348.

3. Clipping file (Theatres: U.S.: New York: American Concert Hall), Billy Rose Theatre Collection, New York Public Library at Lincoln Center, and *Spirit of the Times*, 10 February 1860.

4. *New York Herald*, 16 January 1860, 7.

5. *Spirit of the Times*, 21 August 1869, 16, and 28 August 1869, 32.

6. *New York Herald*, 27 February 1860, 7, and 11 March 1860, 7.

7. Maud and Otis Skinner, eds. *One Man in His Time: The Adventures of H. Watkins Strolling Player 1845–1863* (Philadelphia: University of Pennsylvania Press, 1938), 237, 245.

8. *New York Dramatic Mirror*, 2 May 1891, 7.

9. *Spirit of Times*, 21 April 1860, 132, and 5 May 1860, 156. Emma Brougham had previously managed a theatre in Richmond, England, where Laura Keene made her stage debut according to the *Spirit of the Times*, 8 November 1962, 149. She later acted at Laura Keene's Theatre in New York.

10. Ibid., 19 September 1863, 37.

11. Gordon Samples, *Lust for Fame: The Stage Career of John Wilkes Booth* (Jefferson, N. C.: McFarland and Company, 1982), 85. The only other New York appearance was in a special performance of *Julius Caesar* with his brothers on 25 November 1864 at the Winter Garden.

12. *Spirit of the Times*, 19 April 1862, 112.

13. See ibid., 23 January 1864, 345, 10 December 1864, 235, and 3 June 1865, 221, for mention of Provost's illnesses.

14. *Spirit of the Times*, 9 July 1864, 304.

15. Clement Scott, *The Drama of Yesterday and To-day* (London: Macmillan and Company, 1899), 1:138, and Charlotte M. Martin, ed., *The Stage Reminiscences of Mrs. Gilbert* (New York: Charles Scribner's Sons, 1901), 78.

16. Catherine Mary Reignolds-Winslow, *Yesterdays with Actors* (Boston: Cupples and Company, 1887), 115–16.

17. Olympic Theatre Account Book, 1864–65, Rare Books and Manuscript Division, Research Libraries, New York Public Library.

18. J. H. Stoddart, *Recollections of a Player* (New York: The Century Company, 1902), 143–44.

19. *Spirit of the Times*, 7 July 1866, 304.

20. Ibid., 17 March 1869, 96.

21. Ibid., 1 May 1869, 176.

22. *Brooklyn Daily Eagle*, 2 April 1864, 2.

23. Ibid., 29 April 1875, 2.

24. There is general agreement in the press and by historians that Sarah Conway managed with little assistance from her husband, whose deteriorating

health prevented him from even acting nightly with the company. The *Brooklyn Daily Eagle*, 17 July 1875, 4, reported that "it is no secret that for several years before the retirement of her husband from the stage, she managed the theatre exclusively." In 1923 two letters appeared in the *Sun* (New York) from men who had attended Mrs. Conway's theatre in their youth. They both commented on Mrs. Conway's business aptitude. William F. Hammond, on 26 May 1923, wrote that Mr. Conway "left the business management of the theatre to his wife, who possessed undoubted executive ability." Apparently, the unusual situation of the wife, rather than the husband, running the family business made a strong impression upon the young theatregoers, who clearly recalled the arrangement fifty years later. A copy of the letter from Hammond is in the Sarah Conway clipping file, Billy Rose Theatre Collection, New York Public Library at Lincoln Center. A copy of the other letter, dated 27 April 1923, is in the Sarah Conway clipping file, Harvard Theatre Collection.

25. See, for example, the *Brooklyn Daily Eagle*, 10 September 1866, 2, which reported, "The musicians behaved abominably. They missed all their cues in the first act and came trooping into the orchestra in disorderly fashion, in the middle of the performance and spoiling the effect of the fine soliloquy."

26. Ibid., 13 April 1864, 2.

27. Ibid.

28. *Brooklyn Daily Eagle*, 25 October 1867, 2.

29. *Spirit of the Times*, 28 March 1874, 159.

30. *Brooklyn Daily Eagle*, 13 October 1865, 2.

31. Ibid., 23 April 1867, 2.

32. *Spirit of the Times*, 28 March 1874, 159.

33. Unidentified clipping in Harvard clipping file dated 18 February 1876.

34. For accounts of the legal battle for control of the Brooklyn Theatre, see especially the *Brooklyn Daily Eagle*, 6 July 1875 and the *New York Herald*, 18 July 1875.

35. Phyllis Hartnoll, *The Oxford Companion to the Theatre*, 2d ed. (London: Oxford University Press, 1957), 785, and the *New York Dramatic Mirror*, 4 July 1891.

36. T. Allston Brown, *History of the American Stage* (1870; reprint, New York: Burt Franklin, 1969), 323. Apparently, the purchasing of debuts was a fairly common occurance, though most aspiring actresses disappeared after a night or two if not well received.

37. *Spirit of the Times*, 14 October 1865, 112.

38. Mary Henderson, *The City and the Theatre* (Clifton, N. J.: James T. White and Company, 1973), 117.

39. *Spirit of the Times*, 23 December 1865, 272.

40. Ibid., 6 January 1866, 304.

41. Ibid., 17 February 1866, 400.

42. Ibid., 31 March 1866, 80.

43. Ibid., 7 April 1866, 96.

44. Ibid., 14 April 1866, 112.

45. Ibid., 21 April 1866, 128.

46. Ibid., 27 March 1869, 96.

47. Clippings file, Worrell Sisters, Billy Rose Theatre Collection, New York Public Library at Lincoln Center. Irene apparently married, retired from the stage, and moved away from New York.

48. *Brooklyn Daily Eagle*, 19 February 1869, 2.

49. Ibid., 21 December 1868, 2.

50. Ibid., 30 June 1870, 3.

51. *Spirit of the Times*, 5 November 1870, 192.

52. T. Allston Brown, *A History of the New York Stage* (New York: Dodd, Mead and Company, 1903), 1:295.

53. *New York Star*, 2 May 1924, and unidentified clip dated 1919 in Robinson Locke Collection of scrapbooks, Billy Rose Theatre Collection, New York Public Library at Lincoln Center. I have no date for Cummings's possible management of the New Haven Opera House. There is no mention of Minnie Cummings in *The Actors' Fund Association of America: A Brief History of the Foundation of the Fund and Annual Reports 1882–93* (1894) or Louis M. Simon, *A History of the Actors' Fund of America* (New York: Theatre Arts Books, 1972). It is possible, however, that she organized one of the many benefits for indigent actors held before the formation of the Actors' Fund.

54. An unidentified clipping in the Robinson Locke Collection, Billy Rose Theatre Collection, New York Public Library at Lincoln Center, berates Claxton for attempting management in Brooklyn while memory of the great fire lingered.

55. *New York Dramatic Mirror*, 8 December 1894, 2. In fact, an actress did not necessarily receive the same remuneration as an actor, but compared to women in other types of work her prospects were good. Edna Hammer Cooley, in "Women in American Theatre 1850–1870: A Study of Professional Equity." (Ph.D. diss., University of Maryland, 1986), makes interesting observations on theatre salaries in the twenty years preceding Claxton's career. Cooley, working from limited available data, found that when salaries of performers at all levels, utility to leading player, were averaged, women earned 80 percent of men's wages. In other fields where men and women were employed at the same jobs, Cooley found that women typically received only 50 percent of the standard male wage, and were found only in lower status jobs (none equivalent to a leading player). One contributing factor to the not completely equitable pay for actresses was that most companies performing a standard repertory required not only more actors than actresses, but also more men than women in leading parts. Therefore, more men would be higher on the pay scale. However, it was possible for a particular woman to earn as much or more than her fellow actors at the leading player or visiting star level, where box office appeal was the determining factor.

56. "Our Gallery of Players," XXXIV (Helen Dauvray), article in Dauvray clipping file, Theatre Collection, Museum of the City of New York.

57. Daniel Frohman, *Daniel Frohman Presents* (New York: Claude Kendall and Willoughby Sharp, 1935), 62–63.

58. Charles Pike Sawyer, "The Mirror of the Stage: Helen Dauvray as An Actress-Manager—Reflections of Her Career at the Old Lyceum—Her Company," *New York Post* 29 December 1923. Clipping in Dauvray file, Billy Rose Theatre Collection, NewYork Public Library at Lincoln Center.

59. Nym Crinkle, *New York Dramatic Mirror*, 21 September 1889, 1.

60. Unidentified clipping in Rosina Vokes file, Harvard Theatre Collection.

6

Beyond the Theatrical Centers—Later Nineteenth-Century Women Theatre Managers throughout the United States

During the second half of the nineteenth century women managed theatres in many parts of the United States besides New York City and Philadelphia, but they did not receive as much attention as their peers, and their activities are not always as well documented. This chapter will present information on several women managers to demonstrate the existence of women in theatre management throughout the country. It seems likely that other women who managed theatres, especially in small communities or for short periods of time, remain to be discovered.

JANE ENGLISH

Mrs. Jane English, who presented a summer season at Laura Keene's Theatre in 1863, also managed a theatre of her own in Boston. Better known as the mother of Lucille and Helen Western, Jane, after the death of Mr. Western, had married theatrical manager William B. English, who actively promoted the stage careers of his stepdaughters. Early in 1863 Jane English undertook her own management venture, leasing Allston Hall on Tremont Street in Boston and opening it in February as the New Tremont Street Theatre. Possibly William English, who died on 30 July 1864 and may have been ill before that time, encouraged his actress-wife to take up his profession in order better to support herself.

Although Jane English was not successful in establishing a permanent theatre, she took her company, named the Troupe St. Denis, on the road, presenting variety entertainment by vocalists, acrobats, pantomimists, and dancers. From May to July 1863 her troupe resided in the New York City theatre previously known as Laura Keene's Theatre. On 18 July 1863 the *Spirit of the Times* announced that she planned to resume management of the Tremont Street Theatre with her variety troupe for the winter.[1] If English returned to the Tremont Street Theatre at all, it was only for a short visit. Instead, she toured extensively with her company during the 1863–64 season, visiting Alexandria, Buffalo, Louisville, Memphis, St. Louis, Cairo, Nashville, and Cincinnati.[2] English apparently dissolved her troupe in the summer of 1864. She later was in the costuming business for a time before her death in October 1898.[3]

JULIA BENNETT BARROW

Another woman, Julia Bennett Barrow, managed Boston's Tremont Street Theatre for a short time after Jane English. Prior to this time, Barrow, a popular comic actress, had been part of a management team at Boston's Howard Athenaeum. She and her husband, Jacob Barrow, assumed control of the Howard Athenaeum on 1 March 1858. He had served as acting manager from 6 July to 7 August 1857, with E. L. Davenport as stage manager, and as lessee and manager from 11 to 29 August, with H. Ashley as acting manager.[4] Julia Bennett Barrow acted at the Howard Athenaeum for only the first ten nights of her husband's initial managerial stint, before leaving to honor other engagements. During the Barrows' partnership the bills proclaimed that the theatre was "Under the Direction of Mrs. Barrow," with sole lessee and manager Jacob Barrow and stage manager Henry Wallack.[5] This management, which lasted through October 1858, presented a season weighted toward comedy and starring Julia Barrow.

Beyond the billing, it is not clear how the Barrows divided managerial responsibility. Contemporary newspaper accounts credit Julia Barrow with the management of the theatre: "She took one of the most agreeable, yet most neglected theatres in the country [and] spared neither labor nor expense towards its renovation" and "The success of the Howard Athenaeum company, under the direction of Mrs. Barrow, continues full tide."[6] Having toured for several years as the head of an acting company, Julia Bennett Barrow briefly managed the Tremont Street Theatre in Boston early in 1864.[7]

MRS. T. B. LOGAN AND MRS. HARRY HUNTER

Women also managed theatres in newer, less populated cities with shorter theatrical histories than Boston. Galveston, Texas, for example had two women theatre managers. Mrs. T. B. (Ada) Logan, who had been acting in Galveston by 1852, was the first person to reestablish theatrical activity in that city after it was shut down by a yellow fever epidemic in the fall of 1858. Leasing and refitting the local theatre in January 1859, Mrs. Logan received encouragement from the *News* (Galveston), which wrote, "We have been so long without anything at all respectable in that line that a play well acted will prove a great treat indeed.''[8] Beginning on 22 January 1859, Mrs. Logan's company presented popular pieces, such as *The Hunchback*, *The Rough Diamond*, *Still Waters Run Deep*, *The Lady of Lyons*, and *Lucretia Borgia*. When her benefit was announced for 25 March 1859, the local paper predicted a good house for the woman who had done much "to establish the drama on a legitimate basis in this city."[9] On 20 April 1859 Logan moved her troupe to Houston, opening on 25 April at the Lone Star Hall. The length of her engagement there is unknown.

Another woman managing the Galveston Theatre for a season was Mrs. Harry Hunter, who produced several plays including *The Spectre Bridegroom*, *Ingomar*, *Green Bushes*, *Romeo and Juliet*, and *Leah, the Forsaken* in April and May 1867.

MRS. H. A. PERRY

In 1861 Mrs. H. A. Perry managed a season at the Metropolitan Theatre in Detroit. After she gained fame as the actress Agnes Booth, however, her early managerial career was almost completely forgotten. Born Marion Agnes Laud in Sydney, Australia, in 1843, she was performing in San Francisco with her sister Belle by 1858. Marrying the comic actor Harry Perry in 1860, she began to perform under the name Mrs. H. A. Perry. From 30 September through 25 December 1861 (possibly through January 1862) she was lessee and manager of the Metropolitan Theatre in Detroit. Visiting stars at Mrs. H. A. Perry's Metropolitan Theatre included J. H. Hackett, Sallie St. Clair, Maggie Mitchell, John Wilkes Booth, Kate Bateman, and Ada Isaacs Menken.[10] H.A. Perry died in late 1861 or early 1862, and his sudden death was possibly a factor in the end of his wife's management. Continuing her acting career, Mrs. Perry toured in Ohio and then in Nevada, before moving to the East Coast in 1865 and marrying Junius Brutus Booth, Jr.

Although newspaper accounts of the life of Agnes Booth frequently refer to her early marriage, they do not mention her management of Detroit's Metropolitan Theatre. Perhaps Agnes Booth considered her brief management career less than distinguished and so did not mention it to reporters. The absence of any mention of her early management is particularly striking, however, because several newspaper articles note her interest in managing a theatre. It was reported that she would love to have her own theatre if she could afford it.[11] After the death of Junius Booth, Jr., in 1883, Agnes married theatre manager John B. Schoeffel and ventured into management on a small scale, producing occasional open-air Shakespeare productions at their home in Manchester, Massachusetts, as charity benefits.[12]

MISS A. G. TRIMBLE

In Albany, New York, the Academy of Music came under the management of a woman in 1867. Originally built as the South Pearl Street Theatre in 1825, the Academy of Music had been converted to a church from 1839 to 1862, before theatre architect John Trimble, retired due to blindness, reopened it as a theatre on 28 December 1863.[13] Trimble died on 7 June 1867 and his daughter, Miss A. G. Trimble, assumed the management. Albany historian H.P. Phelps reported:

> On account of her father's infirmity and the belief that there were some persons in the world not too good to rob a blind man, she had for some months previous to Mr. Trimble's death, been his constant attendant in the box office, and aided him all that she could, even to counting the house. As he grew more feeble, and felt that his end was approaching, he asked her to undertake the management when he was gone. Reluctant to assume such a responsibility, she tried to think of some other way, but none appeared. There was no one else to do it, and, of course, she consented. Contracts had already been made with a number of stars, and these were carried out, and new ones entered into. In short, the season under this enterprising and plucky little manager...netted her $8,000.[14]

Miss Trimble's season ran from 2 September 1867 until 29 January 1868, when a fire destroyed the theatre, at an estimated loss of $40,000.[15] Retiring from management, Trimble married Lucien Barnes, manager from 1869 to 1872 of the Trimble Opera House, named in honor of her father.

ELIZABETH MAGILL

Women theatre managers—for example, Laura Keene and Mrs. John Drew—were active in northern states during the Civil War, but they also had southern counterparts, who, though not nearly as prominent, had rather remarkable careers. Mrs. Elizabeth Magill earned the appreciation of her fellow citizens when she built the New Richmond Theatre to replace Hewitt's Theatre in Richmond, which had burned down on New Year's Day, 1863. Opening on 9 February 1863, the New Richmond was a full-size, new building, not a small converted space, and it boasted some form of theatrical entertainment through Lee's surrender on 9 April 1865. Writing about the theatre in 1955, R. B. Harwell claimed that Elizabeth Magill was the owner while Mr. R. d'Orsey Ogden was the manager.[16] Of course, it is possible that Ogden was simply the stage manager, for a newspaper account from 1875 recalled that Magill had been both proprietor and manager, asserting that the "better classes" in Richmond had not attended the theatre since the time of her management.[17]

VIRGINIA KEMBLE

Virginia Kemble was an actress who came out of retirement early in 1864 to join a theatrical company headed by Edmund Dalton, which played in Savannah, Augusta, and Macon, Georgia. The Dalton troupe played at Macon's Ralston's Hall, which by late summer 1864 remained the only legitimate theatre in operation in Georgia. On 3 September 1864 the troupe disbanded, but Virginia Kemble assembled a new company and reopened Ralston's Hall on 8 September. Presenting programs of light comedies, farces, singing, and dancing, she kept her theatre open (though it was in Sherman's path from Atlanta to Savannah) until 18 April 1865, after the Confederate government had fled Richmond and just two days before Macon was captured by Union cavalry.[18]

ROSE THOMPSON

In Memphis, Tennessee, which was captured by the Union Army on 6 June 1862, the New Memphis Theatre was seized by the federal government, leaving manager William C. Thompson without a theatre until he was allowed to return to his post in 1865. During his hiatus, he presumably had reason to be thankful for the millinery and French goods store near the theatre (hopefully, well stocked before the war), run by his wife, Rose. Occupied with her own business, Rose Thompson only gradually began to participate in the management of the New Memphis. One of her earliest theatrical undertakings was to supervise a group of women who presented a series of tableaux to benefit wounded soldiers on 27 November 1861. Beginning in January 1867 she assumed a large part of the managerial responsibilities along with the theatre's treasurer, Chris P. Steinkuhl, when William Thompson became ill. One of her tasks was to rehearse the fifty young women hired as a ballet corps for a production of *The Black Crook*, which opened on 10 February 1868. Rose Thompson officially assumed the management of the New Memphis Theatre after the death of her husband on 10 August 1868.[19]

Thompson opened the new season on 15 October 1868, after traveling to New York City with Steinkuhl to engage actors. She followed her husband's policy of presenting a stock company supplemented by stars, which for the 1868–69 season included Charlotte Thompson, Lotta Crabtree, Maggie Mitchell, Frank Mayo, and Joseph Proctor. Despite the presence of star attractions, Thompson found it difficult to make money, probably because of the high salaries required to attract such performers. On 17 November 1868 the *Memphis Daily Appeal* encouraged the public not to spend all their entertainment money on Friday nights, the visiting star benefit nights at the New Memphis, because Thompson would not receive the proceeds.[20]

In an effort to boost business Thompson produced a number of spectacular pieces, but this policy raised her costs without significantly improving business. Beginning in January 1869 she faced new troubles in the form of competition from David Bidwell and Gilbert Spaulding, who began producing plays at Greenlaw's Opera House. The disappointing 1868–69 season at the New Memphis Theatre ended on an even worse note when the final visiting attraction, the Whitman Opera Company led by Benjamin Whitman, skipped town, leaving a debt of $2,000 to $3,000.[21] Deciding to return to shopkeeping, Rose Thompson gave up the lease to the New Memphis Theatre, which was then taken over by Spaulding and Bidwell.[22]

MRS. DAVID BIDWELL

Twenty years after Rose Thompson's final season as a manager, David Bidwell became seriously ill. His wife assumed managerial duties at the beginning of the 1888–89 season for the two theatres still controlled by Bidwell: the St. Charles Theatre and the Academy of Music, both in New Orleans. After Bidwell's death on 18 December 1889, Mrs. Bidwell formally assumed ownership and management of the theatres. Because both were operated as combination houses by this point, her primary responsibility was to book attractions. Mrs. Bidwell was moderately successful operating the St. Charles Theatre as a popular-price house with appearances by Mary Ten Broeck, Maude Atkinson, John Henshaw, James O'Neill, Joseph Jefferson, and Mrs. John Drew, as well as lesser known "stars." At the end of the 1892–93 season she retired from management, leasing her theatres to the theatrical syndicate of Jefferson, Klaw, and Erlanger. Mrs. Bidwell died in May 1897 at age 64.[23]

MRS. FRANK S. (HENRIETTA) CHANFRAU

Another New Orleans theatre managed by a woman was the Varieties. The Variété Association conducted a search for a new manager for the 1875–76 season, following the departure of John Owens, and invited Mrs. Frank S. Chanfrau to take the position.[24] Mrs. Chanfrau had been born Henrietta Baker in 1837 in New Jersey and began acting as a teenager in Philadelphia and Cincinnati. Marrying Frank Chanfrau on 23 June 1858, she made her first New York appearance at Wallack's Theatre in August 1858 with her husband.[25] The Chanfraus apparently pursued their separate careers and made little effort to act together, or even to work in the same city. By 1875 Mrs.

Chanfrau had appeared several times in New Orleans and was quite popular with local audiences. She made a brief tour supported by company members from the Varieties before opening the theatre in December 1875 with Clifton W. Tayleure's *Parted; or, The Bank Failure*. Tayleure was appointed business manager of the Varieties by Chanfrau, who had previously toured extensively in Tayleure's *A Woman's Wrongs* and had hired him as her personal business agent.[26] Chanfrau managed the Varieties for just one season, which seems to have lasted only through February 1859. In later years, after leaving the stage, Henrietta Chanfrau purchased the *Long Branch News (New Jersey)* and reportedly was a leader in the Christian Science movement.[27]

MRS. JOHN FOREPAUGH

Late in the century, another woman manager appeared in Philadelphia. Mrs. John Forepaugh took over the management of the Forepaugh Family Theatre when her husband became ill in 1895 and continued to manage it until 1902. The Forepaugh was a "popular price" stock company, providing inexpensive entertainment for a local audience by securing the rights to plays after they had been produced by touring combination companies. Mrs. Forepaugh typically advertised each play as "another $1.50 production seen at this theatre for 10, 20, 30, or 50 cents."[28] The *Philadelphia Inquirer* reported as she began the 1895–96 season that "Mrs. John A. Forepaugh is demonstrating her ability as a theatrical manager by securing the very cream of modern plays which have been produced at the highest priced houses, and which she will present in splendid style at the Forepaugh Family Theatre during the coming season."[29] Not an actress herself, Mrs. Forepaugh concentrated her efforts on staging scenically elaborate productions. She was assisted in her efforts by the company's leading man, George Learock, who from time to time was announced as the stage director of a particular piece.

Mari Kathleen Fielder reports, "Exemplifying the trend of female proprietorship in the regional stock companies, Mrs. Forepaugh brought a keen awareness of female audience tastes and needs as well as a recognition of female influence over entertainment choice to the Forepaugh Stock Company."[30] The appeal to a female audience included daily matinees, reminders in the ads to bring the children, and a repertoire heavily loaded with sentimental and romantic melodramas. Although Mrs. Forepaugh inherited her successful managerial policy, emphasizing one-week runs of proven hit plays at popular prices, she deserves credit for continuing a profitable management for seven more years. She demonstrated an ability to judge which plays would appeal most to her audiences, to secure the rights to these plays at reasonable rates and to mount them effectively.

COMPANY MANAGERS AND OTHERS

Brief mentions of other women suggest an even more extensive presence of women in management. For example, the Louisville Theatre was managed for a time by Miss Leo Hudson, and the Pittsburgh Opera House was managed by Anna Eberle.[31] In Cairo, Illinois, Miss Mary McWilliams was managing the local theatre in January 1864.[32] In March 1865 the *Spirit of the Times* announced that another woman, Mrs. Emma Waller, who had considered becoming the lessee of the Cairo Athenaeum, decided against venturing into management.[33]

In addition to the women who managed individual theatres around the country, many women managed traveling theatre companies. These women arranged engagements with local managers or leased theatres for short periods. Their activities are not the focus of this study, but their presence further indicates that women found many opportunities to assume leadership roles in the American theatre during the nineteenth century.

One successful company manager was Jennie Kimball, an actress who abandoned her own stage career to promote her young daughter Corinne. In 1881 Kimball organized a juvenile opera company starring Corinne. The Society for the Prevention of Cruelty to Children attempted to prevent the company from performing but only succeeded in generating more publicity for Corinne. The Kimball Opera Company toured extensively until Jennie Kimball's death in 1896, when she left her daughter an estate estimated at $600,000.[34]

Other drama, opera, and dance companies led by women included Mrs. Powell's Dramatic Troupe, Miss Dolly Bidwell's Company, the Katie Putnam Comedy Company, Flora Myers's Dramatic Company, the Julie Coventry Dramatic Company, the Kathleen O'Neil Novelty Troupe, the Elise Holt Burlesque Troupe, the Mrs. James A. Oates Company, the Kellogg English Opera Company, Susan Galton's Opera Bouffe Troupe, Madame Kathi Lanner's ballet troupe, Lillian Conway's Opera Company, and many others.[35] This sampling of women managers at various places around the country and those on the road with touring companies suggests that there were significant numbers of women in the management business and much of their activity remains to be explored.

NOTES

1. *Spirit of the Times*, 18 July 1863, 309.
2. Ibid., 29 August 1863 through 18 June 1864.
3. *Boston Herald*, 26 October 1898, obituary in Harvard clipping file.
4. Howard Athenaeum playbills, Harvard Theatre Collection.
5. Howard Athenaeum bill, 1 March 1858, Harvard Theatre Collection.

6. Unidentified clippings in Julia Bennett Barrow file, Harvard Theatre Collection. Years later an article in the *Boston Transcript*, 11 April 1891, reported that Jacob Barrow had been the ostensible director during Mrs. Barrow's management, but this may be just the opinion of one writer working from the assumption that a husband would have had the real authority in any such joint venture.

7. *Spirit of the Times*, 9 January 1864, 293, and *Boston Herald*, 26 October 1898, in Harvard clipping file.

8. *News* (Galveston), 15 January 1859, quoted in Joseph Gallegly, *Footlights on the Border: The Galveston and Houston Stage before 1900* (The Hague: Mouton and Company, 1962), 63. Gallegly is the main source for Logan and Mrs. Harry Hunter.

9. *News* (Galveston), 25 March 1859, quoted in Gallegly, 63.

10. Elaine Elizabeth McDavitt, "A History of the Theatre in Detroit, Michigan, from Its Beginnings to 1862" (Ph.D. diss., University of Michigan, 1946), 379–83.

11. *New York Herald*, 9 February 1889, and other clippings in Agnes Booth file, Billy Rose Theatre Collection, New York Public Library at Lincoln Center.

12. *Spirit of the Times*, 14 July 1888, 221, and clipping labeled *New York Dramatic Mirror*, 8 January 1910, in the Harvard Theatre Collection.

13. Joel Munsell, *Collections on the History of Albany: From Its Discovery to the Present Time, with Notices of Public Institutions, and Biographical Sketches of Citizens Deceased* (Albany, N. Y.: J. Munsell, 1867), 2:35–37.

14. H[enry]. P[itt]. Phelps, *A Record of the Albany Stage* (Albany, N. Y.: Joseph McDonough, 1880), 359.

15. *Spirit of the Times*, 8 February 1868, 444.

16. R. B. Harwell, "Civil War Theatre: The Richmond Stage," *Civil War History* 1 (September 1955): 300. Ogden is also named as manager of the Richmond Theatre in Charles S. Watson, "Confederate Drama: The Plays of John Hill Hewitt and James Dabney McCabe," *Southern Literary Journal* 21 (Spring 1989): 100–112.

17. *Brooklyn Daily Eagle*, 9 March 1875, 2.

18. Iline Fife, "The Confederate Theater in Georgia," *Georgia Review* 9 (Fall 1955): 305–15.

19. Information on Rose Thompson from Seldon Faulkner, "The New Memphis Theatre of Memphis, Tennessee, from 1859 to 1880" (Ph.D. diss., University of Iowa, 1957), and Faulkner entry on the New Memphis Theatre in Weldon B. Durham, ed., *American Theatre Companies, 1749–1887* (New York: Greenwood Press, 1986), 345–51.

20. *Memphis Daily Appeal*, 17 November 1868, quoted in Faulkner, dissertation, 97–98.

21. Faulkner, dissertation, 104.

22. Faulkner in Durham, 349.

23. Information on Mrs. David Bidwell from John S. Kendall, *The Golden Age of the New Orleans Theater* (Baton Rouge: Louisiana State University Press, 1952), 573, and Jo Ann Lawlor, "History of the St. Charles Theatre of New Orleans, 1888–1899," (Master's thesis, Louisiana State University, 1966).

24. Kendall, 450.

25. Unidentified newspaper clipping, Chanfrau file, Harvard Theatre Collection.

26. *Spirit of the Times*, 22 November 1873, 354, and Kendall, 450.

27. Unidentified obituary, Chanfrau file, Harvard Theatre Collection.

28. See, for example, the *Philadelphia Inquirer*, 27 December 1896, 23.

29. Ibid., 14 July 1895, 4.

30. Mari Kathleen Fielder, "Forepaugh Stock Company," in Weldon B. Durham, ed., *American Theatre Companies 1888–1930* (New York: Greenwood Press, 1987), 172.

31. Helen Waverly Deutsch, "Laura Keene's Theatre Management: Profile of a Profession in Transition" (Ph.D. diss., Tufts University, 1992), 243.

32. *Spirit of the Times*, 23 January 1864, 325.

33. Ibid., 4 March 1865, 16.

34. *New York Dramatic Mirror*, 4 April 1896, 2, and Jennie Kimball clipping file, Billy Rose Theatre Collection, New York Public Library at Lincoln Center.

35. Activities of these companies reported in the *Spirit of the Times*.

Conclusion

Throughout the nineteenth century women held leadership positions in the American theatre, working as theatre managers. Some, such as Laura Keene and Mrs. John Drew, reached the top of the profession. Many others enjoyed moderate success without ever becoming influential or widely known. Some assumed the management of a theatre after the death of a husband or father. Others turned to management in order to showcase their own acting, especially when other managers did not wish to feature them. After a season or two many women decided that management was less profitable or more effort than they had imagined and made their exit. There were also some women who clearly failed as managers, but even their efforts demonstrate the ambitions of nineteenth-century American women to enter the competitive business.

As both actresses and managers, women found the theatre to be an attractive profession during the nineteenth century. Unlike in many fields of employment, women were not barred or kept in the lowest ranks, for plays required leading women as well as leading men. In the theatre a woman could earn a living and find an outlet for artistic expression. If she had talent, persistence, and good luck, she might even acquire wealth and fame. For a woman who entered theatre management the potential rewards were even greater. Her control extended to every aspect of production, including play selection, role assignment, and choice of costumes, scenery, and music. As a manager a woman was not only part of the work force, but an employer. Although throughout the century it remained unusual for any woman to be in a position to hire, train, supervise, and discipline men, these things were done by women managers. The entrepreneurial aspect of their work also distinguished theatre managers from other nineteenth-century working women, a majority of whom labored as unskilled factory workers or carried out domestic tasks, such as cooking, cleaning, and sewing. The theatre manager assumed financial risks, but gained the potential of large profits. She also had the satisfaction of making her own decisions and meeting the challenge of her work.

Self-reliant, energetic women assumed management positions under a variety of circumstances, which were reflected in their differing managerial styles and levels of success.   If not all women managers achieved the prominence of Laura Keene, it was partially due to the fact that many had aims other than establishing a top New York theatre.   Some managed a theatre only as a temporary measure to create employment or to promote their own acting careers.   Others considered themselves successful if they were simply able to continue the normal existence of a theatre started by a deceased husband. Location was also a factor in the type of management undertaken and in the potential national reputation of a manager.   Laura Keene and Mrs. John Drew reached a degree of fame working in New York and Philadelphia that would have been unlikely if their theatres had been in Detroit or Louisville.   Even a location just slightly removed from a theatrical center could present an entirely different set of circumstances.   Working in Brooklyn, for example, Sarah Conway was unable to follow the New York trend of long-running productions, needing to change bills frequently to meet the demands of her local audience.

The earliest women managers in the United States, Margaretta Sully West and Anne Brunton Merry, inherited the management of a company from their husbands.   Other women also turned to management because it was a family enterprise.   Frances Anne Denny Drake shared managerial duties with her husband and later assisted her aging father-in-law by taking over the management of his theatre.   Elizabeth Richardson took up management for a short time in order to provide several family members with employment.   Later in the century Miss A. G. Trimble carried on the management of her father's theatre after his death, while Mrs. Thompson, Mrs. Bidwell, and Mrs. Forepaugh all became managers following the death of their husbands.

Other women entered management of their own initiative, but early in the century they tended to manage rather small-scale operations that did not attract much notice.   In New York City, for example, Charlotte Baldwin, Elizabeth Hamblin, Annette Nelson, and Virginia Monier managed small theatres with the primary aim of creating an acting opportunity for themselves, rather than with the intention of providing serious competition to the more established theatres.   Not until the 1850s in California were circumstances favorable enough to attract a cluster of women managers, some with ambitious plans. Sarah Kirby Stark, Catherine Sinclair, Rowena Granice, Laura Keene, Mrs. John Wood, Mrs. Woodward, and Miss Goodard are all known to have managed theatres in California.   Stark played an important role in providing theatre for the new audience created by the Gold Rush, while Sinclair's management was significant for raising California entertainment to a new level of sophistication.   Granice demonstrated enterprise in providing amusements for a rowdier crowd.

Attempting to establish themselves in prominent managerial positions, women did meet some resistance. As the first woman to attempt to manage a large, competitive, first-class theatre in New York, Laura Keene encountered more opposition than did most other women. Attacks on her character were printed in local newspapers before her management was even underway; scenery for her first play was slashed, forcing opening night to be delayed; and at the end of her first season her theatre was bought out from under her by a rival manager. Once Keene proved herself to be a capable manager, however, other women were able to attempt management in New York with far less resistance, although, of course, some also faced obstacles. Elizabeth Bowers was so discouraged in her major effort at management that she issued a statement warning other women against such an endeavor. Three women, Matilda Clarendon, Madame de Marguerittes, and Rowena Granice, in widely varying locations and circumstances, even found they had to defend physically the right to manage their theatres.

Among the several women who became managers in New York after Keene cleared the way, the most notable were Mrs. John Wood, who assumed management of Keene's old theatre, renamed the Olympic, and Sarah Conway, who established the first resident stock company in Brooklyn. Keene's success may have helped ease Mrs. John Drew's entry into management, because her work was discussed by the stockholders board that considered inviting Drew to manage the Arch Street Theatre. Drew probably also benefited from the fact that Philadelphia had previously seen several women managers, including Mary Elizabeth Maywood, Charlotte Cushman, Elizabeth Bowers, and Mrs. M. A. Garrettson. With her long, distinguished career as a manager, Drew represents the highest achievement among nineteenth-century women theatre managers.

Beyond Philadelphia and New York City, the large theatrical centers where Drew and Keene became famous, women managed theatres in various parts of the country. Mrs. H. A. Perry, later better known as Agnes Booth, was the manager of the Metropolitan Theatre in Detroit. In New Orleans Ann Sefton managed the American Theatre, and thirty years later in that city Mrs. Frank Chanfrau managed the Varieties. During the Civil War the Confederate states had two women managers, Elizabeth Magill in Richmond and Virginia Kemble in Macon. Women also worked throughout the country as managers of traveling companies.

In sum, considering the social pressure on women to restrict their activities to the domestic sphere, a surprisingly large number of women managed theatres during the nineteenth century. Legal restrictions on a married woman's ability to control her own property and earnings and to enter into contracts was a liability for women trying to enter the professional or business world, but did not prevent them from running their own theatres. While women fought tremendous battles for access to professions such as law and medicine, the theatre in the United States was open to them. Even at the esteemed level of theatre manager, women could find opportunities, and they usually met with little or no apparent opposition. Perhaps this was because women already filled an important role in the theatre as leading players. Also, as theatre people tended to work and live within their own community, they may have been less concerned with assumptions of the larger society that women should not manage business enterprises. Overall, the nineteenth-century American theatre provided unique challenges and opportunities for a number of ambitious women who took on the role of theatre manager.

For the most part, these women managed theatres no differently than men did. They presented the same plays or kind of plays as their male counterparts. Despite the existence of a feminist movement in the United States, widely in evidence after the Seneca Falls convention of 1848, women theatre managers did not produce any overtly feminist drama. Even if it had occurred to any of them to create such works, the threat to their commercial viability would have been a strong inducement to avoid unnecessary controversy. The few plays produced during the nineteenth century advocating women's suffrage were performed almost exclusively as home theatricals.[1] Women managers also worked in the same theatrical spaces as other managers. If some managed in small theatres or converted halls, it was more a matter of economy than aesthetic principle. When women managers hired stars to play at their theatres, they hired the same stars that were popular at houses managed by men. Faced with the same casting requirements as men, women managers hired more men than women as performers, and there is no evidence that women managers made any attempt to increase the number of women working on their support staffs. It was not their goal to attempt to forge an alternative to the existing commercial theatre or to alter radically current practices, but to work within the system.

In some cases, slight differences in managerial style between men and women managers is evident. Some women managers, for example Mary Elizabeth Maywood, were modest in their promises to the public or, like Matilda Clarendon or Elizabeth Bowers, assumed the persona of "helpless female" in published letters and articles. This approach was intended to appeal to a sense of gallantry on the part of audience members and critics. Unfortunately, the weak and helpless persona was not completely compatible with the vigorous energy, initiative, and responsibility needed for running a theatre. Laura Keene was able to use this tactic effectively, however, by maintaining a strict distinction between her public face and backstage personality. A distinctive strategy sometimes used rather successfully by women managers was to plan bills with the aim of attracting a female audience. Mrs. Forepaugh, for example, often presented melodramas or sentimental plays with sympathetic heroines. By establishing frequent matinees, Laura Keene targeted women, since they were much more likely than men to be free to attend the theatre during the day.

Even when conducting the same managerial tasks as men, however, women managers were likely to be perceived differently by both employees and critics. Actors who disliked taking orders from powerful managers were likely to be even more resentful when the manager was a woman. Giving orders and insisting that all employees attempt to meet their own high standards, managers such as Laura Keene and Mrs. John Drew engaged in behavior that was not frequently demonstrated by women at that time, and, therefore, they were seen as being especially strict and demanding. While developing highly disciplined companies which contributed to their success, both women, almost unavoidably, developed reputations for having an authoritarian manner and sharp temper. As public figures, women managers had to struggle to balance the requirements of management against societal expectations of suitably feminine behavior.

Some of the women who attempted management failed, as did hundreds of men around the country who took a chance on the risky business of theatre management—and, by and large, for similar reasons. Those women who did succeed had many attributes in common with the men who did well, such as enormous energy, determination, and awareness of public taste.

Clearly, individual women managers made their share of contributions to the American theatre of the nineteenth century. In California, for example, Sarah Kirby Stark was one of the first managers to start a theatre, opening the Tehama with J. B. Atwater in 1850. Catherine Sinclair was responsible for raising the production standards and cultivating a market for high-class entertainment in the western theatre. The first permanent stock theatre in Brooklyn was established by Sarah Conway, who managed for eleven years until her early death. Widely recognized as an important manager, Laura Keene made regular matinee performances popular and helped establish the trend toward long runs with productions such as *Our American Cousin* and *The Seven Sisters*. Keene's reputation was also based in part on the spectacular staging and elaborate scenery regularly presented at her theatre. Mrs. John Drew had a remarkably long career as a manager and kept up the stock company tradition for many years. Of all the American men and women theatre managers, she was considered one of the best trainers of actors. Establishing her theatre as a successful comedy house, Mrs. John Wood made a daring career move, leaving New York after three seasons of management, while at the height of her popularity, to begin a management career in London. Though sometimes the contribution of a woman manager was simply to meet the demand for entertainment by getting up a show at a particular time and place, individual women were able to achieve success comparable to that of men.

Considered as a group, women theatre managers made still another significant contribution to the American theatre. The history of women managers, along with that of women playwrights and the many actresses, demonstrates clearly that women were active participants in the development of the American theatre throughout the nineteenth century. As visible examples of women in responsible positions, women managers also made a special contribution beyond the theatre. It is even possible—although definite evidence is lacking—that they provided role models for other women who aspired to run a business or direct their own careers. Further, more admired than feared, many of these managers demonstrated that women could perform traditionally male work without suffering a loss of their "feminine" grace, charm, or dignity.

Theatre management during the nineteenth century was a difficult, even discouraging, business, which required long and unusual hours and constant attention. For a woman to succeed in undertaking such a nontraditional occupation, great persistence was necessary. If the theatre tended to be a separate and closed society, the manager struggling to assert her authority over a company was likely to feel isolated within that small world. Other managers in the area were likely to be viewed as rivals, rather than peers. The manager's isolation, therefore, was compounded for a woman, who in some instances would not even have known another woman manager. Theatre management also involved the pressure of continual public scrutiny, with every problem from shabby scenery to ill-rehearsed actors to unfriendly front-of-house staff resulting in potential criticism of the manager. Despite the hardships, many nineteenth-century women demonstrated admirable ambition in accepting the challenge of managing their own theatres.

NOTE

1. See the introduction of Bettina Friedl's *On to Victory: Propaganda Plays of the Woman Suffrage Movement* (Boston: Northeastern University Press, 1987).

Bibliography

BOOKS

Abbott, Edith. *Women in Industry: A Study in American Economic History.* New York: D. Appleton and Company, 1910. Reprint. New York: Arno Press and the New York Times, 1969.

Adelman, Joseph. *Famous Women: An Outline of Feminine Achievement through the Ages with Life Stories of Five Hundred Noted Women.* New York: Ellis M. Lonow Company, 1926.

Alcott, Louisa May. *Work: A Story of Experience.* Boston: Roberts Brothers, 1886.

Archer, Stephan M. *American Actors and Actresses: A Guide to Information Sources.* Detroit: Gale Research Company, 1983.

Auster, Albert. *Actresses and Suffragists: Women in the American Theatre 1890–1920.* New York: Praeger, 1984.

Ayres, Alfred [Thomas E. Osmun]. *Acting and Actors, Elocution and Elocutionists: A Book about Theater Folk and Theater Art.* New York: D. Appleton and Company, 1894.

Baker, Michael. *The Rise of the Victorian Actor.* London: Croom Helm, 1978.

Barnes, J[ohn] H. *Forty Years on the Stage: Others (Principally) and Myself.* London: Chapman and Hall Ltd., 1914.

Barnhart, Jacqueline Baker. *The Fair but Frail: Prostitution in San Franisco 1849–1900.* Reno: University of Nevada Press, 1986.

Barrymore, Ethel. *Memories: An Autobiography.* New York: Harper and Brothers, 1955.

Barrymore, Lionel. *We Barrymores.* New York: Appleton-Century-Crofts, 1951.

Basch, Norma. *In the Eyes of the Law: Women, Marriage and Property in Nineteenth-Century New York*. Ithaca, N. Y.: Cornell University Press, 1982.

Berg, Barbara. *The Remembered Gate: Origins of American Feminism; The Woman and the City, 1800–1860*. New York: Oxford University Press, 1978.

Bernheim, Alfred L. *The Business of the American Theatre: An Economic History of the American Theatre, 1750–1932*. New York: Actors Equity Association, 1932. Reprint. New York: Benjamin Blom, 1964.

Blanc, Marie Therese. *The Condition of Women in the United States*. Boston: Roberts Brothers, 1895.

Bode, Carl, ed. *Midcentury America*. Carbondale: Southern Illinois University Press, 1972.

Bodeen, DeWitt. *Ladies of the Footlights*. Pasadena, Calif.: Pasadena Playhouse Association, 1937.

Bodichon, Barbara Leigh Smith. *Women and Work*. New York: C. S. Francis and Company, 1859.

Brown, T. Allston. *History of the American Stage*. 1870. Reprint. New York: Burt Franklin, 1969.

———. *A History of the New York Stage*. 3 vols. New York: Dodd, Mead and Company, 1903.

Brownlee, W. Elliot and Mary M. *Women in the American Economy: A Documentary History, 1675 to 1929*. New Haven: Yale University Press, 1976.

Bryan, George B. *Stage Lives*. Westport, Conn.: Greenwood Press, 1985.

Buhle, Mari Jo, Ann D. Gordon, and Nancy E. Schrom. *Women in American Society*. Andover, Mass.: Manuscript Modular Publications, 1973.

Campbell, Helen. *Women Wage Earners*. Boston: Roberts Brothers, 1893.

Carroll, Berenice A., ed. *Liberating Women's History: Theoretical and Critical Essays*. Urbana: University of Illinois Press, 1976.

"Case No. 7644, Keene v. Wheatley et al." In *The Federal Cases: Circuit and District Courts of the United States*. Vol. 14. St Paul: West Publishing Company, 1895.

Chinoy, Helen Krich, and Linda Walsh Jenkins, eds. *Women in American Theatre*. New York: Crown Publishers, 1981.

Clapp, Henry Austin. *Reminiscences of a Dramatic Critic*. New York: Houghton Mifflin Company, 1902.

Clapp, John B., and Edwin F. Edgett. *Players of the Present*. 3 vols. New York: Dunlap Society, 1899–1901.

Clarke, M[ary]. *A Concise History of the Life and Amours of Thomas S. Hamblin, Late Manager of the Bowery Theatre, As Communicated by His Legal Wife, Mrs. Elizabeth Hamblin, to Mrs. M. Clarke*. Philadelphia and New York, n. d.

Clinton, Catherine. *The Other Civil War: American Women in the Nineteenth Century*. New York: Hill and Wang, 1984.

Coad, Oral Sumner, and Edwin Mims. *The American Stage*. Vol. 14 of *The Pageant of America*. New Haven: Yale University Press, 1929.

Cogan, Frances B. *All-American Girl: The Ideal of Real Womanhood in Mid-Nineteenth-Century America*. Athens: University of Georgia Press, 1989.

Conway, Jill K. *The Female Experience in 18th and 19th Century America: A Guide to the History of American Women*. Princeton, N. J.: Princeton University Press, 1985.

Cowell, Joe. *Thirty Years Passed among the Players in England and America*. New York: Harper and Brothers, 1844.

Crawford, Mary Caroline. *The Romance of the American Theatre*. Boston: Little, Brown and Company, 1913.

Creahan, John. *The Life of Laura Keene*. Philadelphia: Rogers Publishing Company, 1897.

Dale, Alan [Alfred J. Cohen]. *Familiar Chats with the Queens of the Stage*. New York: G. W. Dillingham, 1890.

Daly, Joseph Francis. *The Life of Augustin Daly*. New York: Macmillan Company, 1917.

Davidge, William. *Footlight Flashes*. New York: American News Company, 1866.

Dexter, Elisabeth Anthony. *Career Women of America 1776–1840*. 1950. Reprint. Clifton, N.J.: Augustus M. Kelley, 1972.

———. *Colonial Women of Affairs before 1776*. 1931. Reprint. Clifton, N.J.: Augustus M. Kelley, 1972.

Dimmick, Ruth Crosby. *Our Theatre To-day and Yesterday*. New York: H. K. Fly Company, 1913.

Donnelly, Mabel Collins. *The American Victorian Woman: The Myth and the Reality*. New York: Greenwood Press, 1986.

Donohue, Joseph W., Jr., ed. *The Theatrical Manager in England and America; Player of a Perilous Game: Philip Henslowe, Tate Wilkinson, Stephen Price, Edwin Booth, Charles Wyndham*. Princeton, N. J.: Princeton University Press, 1971.

Dorland, W[illiam]. A. Newman. *The Sum of Feminine Achievement*. Boston: Stratford Company, 1917.

Doty, Gresdna Ann. *The Career of Mrs. Anne Brunton Merry in the American Theatre*. Baton Rouge: Louisiana State University Press, 1971.

Drew, John. *My Years on the Stage*. New York: E. P. Dutton and Company, 1921.

Drew, Mrs. John [Louisa Lane]. *Autobiographical Sketch of Mrs. John Drew*. New York: Charles Scribner's Sons, 1899.

Dubois, Ellen Carol. *Feminism and Suffrage: The Emergence of an Independent Women's Movement in America, 1848–1869*. Ithaca, N. Y.: Cornell University Press, 1978.

Dudden, Faye E. *Serving Women: Household Service in Nineteenth Century America*. Middleton, Conn.: Wesleyan University Press, 1983.

Durham, Weldon B., ed., *American Theatre Companies 1749–1887*. New York: Greenwood Press, 1986.

———. *American Theatre Companies 1888–1930*. New York: Greenwood Press, 1987.

Edgett, Edwin Francis. *Edward Loomis Davenport*. New York: Dunlap Society, 1901.

Epstein, Barbara Leslie. *The Politics of Domesticity: Women, Evangelism, and Temperance in Nineteenth-Century America*. Middletown, Conn.: Wesleyan University Press, 1981.

Estavan, Lawrence, ed. *San Francisco Theatre Monographs*. W.P.A. Project, 1938–42.

Eytinge, Rose. *The Memories of Rose Eytinge*. New York: Frederick A. Stokes Company, 1905.

Fawkes, Richard. *Dion Boucicault: A Biography*. London: Quartet Books, 1979.

Felheim, Martin. *The Theater of Augustin Daly*. Cambridge: Harvard University Press, 1956.

Flexner, Eleanor. *Century of Struggle: The Women's Rights Movement in the United States*. Rev. ed. Cambridge: Belknap Press of Harvard University, 1975.

Ford, George D. *These Were Actors: A Story of the Chapmans and the Drakes*. New York: Library Publishers, 1955.

Friedl, Bettina. *On to Victory: Propaganda Plays of the Woman Suffrage Movement*. Boston: Northeastern University Press, 1987.

Frohman, Daniel. *Daniel Frohman Presents*. New York: Claude Kendall and Willoughby Sharp, 1935.

Fuller, Margaret. *Woman in the Nineteenth Century*. Boston: John P. Jewett and Company, 1855. Reprint. New York: W. W. Norton and Company, 1970.

Fyles, Franklin. *The Theatre and Its People*. New York: Doubleday, Page and Company, 1900.

Gaer, Joseph, ed. *The Theatre of the Gold Rush Decade in San Francisco*. 1935. Reprint. New York: Burt Franklin, 1970.

Gagey, Edmond M. *The San Francisco Stage*. New York: Columbia University Press, 1950.

Gallegly, Joseph. *Footlights on the Border: The Galveston and Houston Stage before 1900*. The Hague: Mouton and Company, 1962.

Gay, Peter. *Education of the Senses*. vol. 1 of *The Bourgeois Experience: Victoria to Freud*. New York: Oxford University Press, 1984.

Gilder, Rosamond. *Enter the Actress: The First Women in the Theatre*. 1931. Reprint. New York: Theatre Arts Books, 1960.

Gilman, Charlotte Perkins. *Women and Economics: A Study of the Economic Relation between the Men and Women as a Factor in Social Evolution*. Boston: Small, Maynard and Company, 1898. Reprint. Carl W. Degler, ed. New York: Harper and Row, 1966.

Green, Harvey. *The Light of the Home: An Intimate View of the Lives of Women in Victorian America*. New York: Pantheon Books, 1983.

Greever, William S. *The Bonanza West: The Story of the Western Mining Rushes, 1848–1900*. Norman: University of Oklahoma Press, 1963.

Gurko, Miriam. *The Ladies of Seneca Falls: The Birth of the Women's Rights Movement*. New York: Schocken Books, 1976.

Halttunen, Karen. *Confidence Men and Painted Women: A Study of Middle-Class Culture in America, 1830–1870*. New Haven: Yale University Press, 1982.

Harris, Barbara J. *Beyond Her Sphere: Women and the Professions in American History*. Westport, Conn.: Greenwood Press, 1978.

Harrison, Gabriel. "The Progress of the Drama, Opera, Music and Art in Brooklyn." In Henry R. Stiles, ed. *The Civil, Political, Professional, and Ecclesiastical History and Commercial and Industrial Record of the County of Kings and the City of Brooklyn, New York, from 1863 to 1884*. New York: W. W. Munsell, 1884.

Hartnoll, Phyllis. *The Oxford Companion to the Theatre*. 2d ed. London: Oxford University Press, 1957.

Hellerstein, Erna Olafson, Leslie Parker Hume, and Karen M. Offen, eds. *Victorian Women: A Documentary Account of Women's Lives in Nineteenth-Century England, France, and the United States*. Stanford, Calif.: Stanford University Press, 1981.

Henderson, Mary C. *The City and the Theatre: New York Playhouses from Bowling Green to Times Square*. Clifton, N. J.: James T. White and Company, 1973.

Henneke, Ben Graf. *Laura Keene: A Biography*. Tulsa, Okla.: Council Oaks Books, 1990.

Herman, Kali. *Women in Particular: An Index to American Women*. Phoenix: Oryx Press, 1984.

Hill, Joseph. *Women in Gainful Occupations 1870–1920*. Washington, D. C.: U. S. Census Bureau, Census Monographs 9, 1929.

Hill, West T. *The Theatre in Early Kentucky, 1790–1820*. Lexington: University of Kentucky Press, 1971.

Hinding, Andrea, ed. *Women's History Sources: A Guide to Archives and Manuscript Collections in the United States*. 2 vols. New York: R. R. Bowker, 1979.

Hooks, Janet M. *Women's Occupations through Seven Decades*. Women's Bureau Bulletin, no. 218. Washington, D. C.: U. S. Government Printing Office, 1947.

Hornblow, Arthur. *A History of the Theatre in America: From Its Beginnings to the Present Time*. Vol. 2. Philadelphia: J. B. Lippincott Company, 1919.

Howard, Paul, and George Gebbie. *The Stage and Its Stars: Past and Present*. 2 vols. Philadelphia: Gebbie and Company, 1889.

Howe, Daniel Walker, ed. *Victorian America*. Philadelphia: University of Pennsylvania Press, 1976.

Hughes, Glenn. *A History of American Drama 1700–1950*. New York: Samuel French, 1951.

Hutton, Laurence. *Curiosities of the American Stage*. New York: Harper and Brothers, 1891.

―――. *Plays and Players*. New York: Hurd and Houghton, 1875.

Ireland, Joseph N. *Records of the New York Stage from 1750 to 1860*. 2 vols. New York, 1866–67. Reprint. New York: Burt Franklin, 1968.

Irvin, Eric. *Dictionary of the Australian Theatre 1788-1914*. Sydney, Australia: Hale and Iremonger, 1985.

James, Edward T., ed. *Notable American Women 1607–1950: A Biographical Dictionary*. 3 vols. Cambridge: Belknap Press of Harvard University, 1971.

Jefferson, Joseph. *The Autobiography of Joseph Jefferson*. London: T. Fisher Unwin, 1890.

Jennings, John J. *Theatrical and Circus Life: Secrets of the Stage, Green-Room and Saw-Dust Arena*. Chicago: Laird and Lee, 1893.

Johnson, Claudia D. *American Actress: Perspective on the Nineteenth Century*. Chicago: Nelson-Hall, 1984.

Kendall, John S. *The Golden Age of the New Orleans Theater*. Baton Rouge: Louisiana State University Press, 1952.

Kennedy, Susan Estabrook. *If All We Did Was to Weep at Home: A History of White Working-Class Women in America*. Bloomington: Indiana University Press, 1979.

Kerber, Linda K., and Jane DeHart-Mathews, eds. *Women's America: Refocusing the Past*. 2d ed. New York: Oxford University Press, 1987.

Kessler-Harris, Alice. *Out to Work: A History of Wage-Earning Women in the United States*. New York: Oxford University Press, 1982.

Koon, Helene Wickham. *How Shakespeare Won the West: Players and Performances in America's Gold Rush 1849–1865*. Jefferson, N. C.: McFarland and Company, 1989.

Larson, Carl F. W. *American Regional Theatre History to 1900: A Bibliography*. Metuchen, N. J.: Scarecrow Press, 1979.

Leach, Joseph. *Bright Particular Star: The Life and Times of Charlotte Cushman*. New Haven: Yale University Press, 1970.

Leavitt, M. B. *Fifty Years in Theatrical Management, 1859–1909.* New York: Broadway Publishing Company, 1912.

Leman, Walter M. *Memories of an Old Actor.* San Francisco: A. Roman Company, 1886.

Lerner, Gerda. *The Majority Finds Its Past: Placing Women in History.* New York: Oxford University Press, 1979.

Logan, Olive. *Apropos of Women and the Theatre.* New York: Carleton, 1869.

———. *The Mimic World, and Public Exhibitions: Their History, Their Morals, and Effects.* Philadelphia: New World Publishing Company, 1871.

Lotchin, Roger W. *San Francisco 1846–1856: From Hamlet to City.* New York: Oxford University Press, 1974.

Love, Harold, ed., *The Australian Stage: A Documentary History.* Kensington NSW, Australia: New South Wales University Press, 1984.

McArthur, Benjamin. *Actors and American Culture, 1880–1920.* Philadelphia: Temple University Press, 1984.

McKay, Frederic Edward, and Charles E. L. Wingate, eds. *Famous American Actors of To-Day.* New York: Thomas Y. Crowell and Company, 1896.

MacMinn, George R. *The Theatre of the Golden Era in California.* Caldwell, Idaho: Caxton Printers Ltd., 1941.

Marshall, Thomas Frederick. *A History of the Philadelphia Theatre, 1878–1890.* Philadelphia: University of Pennsylvania Press, 1943.

Martin, Charlotte M., ed. *The Stage Reminiscences of Mrs. Gilbert.* New York: Charles Scribner's Sons, 1901.

Matthaei, Julie A. *An Economic History of Women in America: Women's Work, the Sexual Division of Labor, and the Development of Capitalism.* New York: Schocken Books, 1982.

Meserve, Walter J. *American Drama to 1900: A Guide to Information Sources.* Detroit: Gale Research Company, 1980.

———. *Heralds of Promise: The Drama of the American People during the Age of Jackson, 1829–1849.* New York: Greenwood Press, 1986.

Meyer, Annie Nathan. *Woman's Work in America.* New York: H. Holt and Company, 1891.

Moses, Montrose J. *Famous Actor-Families in America.* New York: Thomas Y. Crowell and Company, 1906.

Moyer, Ronald L. *American Actors, 1861–1910: An Annotated Bibliography of Books Published in the United States in English from 1861 through 1976.* Troy, N. Y.: Whitston Publishing Company, 1979.

Mullin, Donald, ed. *Victorian Actors and Actresses in Review: A Dictionary of Contemporary Views of Representative British and American Actors and Actresses, 1837–1901.* Westport, Conn.: Greenwood Press, 1983.

Munsell, Joel. *Collections on the History of Albany: From Its Discovery to the Present Time, with Notices of Public Institutions, and Biographical Sketches of Citizens Deceased.* Vol. 2. Albany, N. Y.: J. Munsell, 1867.

Murdoch, James E. *The Stage.* New York: Benjamin Blom, 1974.

Newton, Judith, Mary P. Ryan, and Judith Walkowitz, eds. *Sex and Class in Women's History.* London: Routledge and Kegan Paul, 1983.

Nicoll, Allardyce. *A History of English Drama 1660–1900.* Vol. 6. *A Short-Title Alphabetical Catalogue of Plays Produced or Printed in England from 1660 to 1900.* 1959. Reprint. Cambridge: Cambridge University Press, 1965.

Odell, George C. D. *Annals of the New York Stage.* 15 vols. New York: Columbia University Press, 1927–41. Reprint. New York: AMS Press, 1970.

Pascoe, Charles E. *Our Actors and Actresses: The Dramatic List.* London: Temple Publishing Company, 1880.

Pemberton, T. Edgar. *A Memoir of Edward Askew Sothern.* 2d ed. London: Richard Bentley and Son, 1889.

Penny, Virginia. *How Women Can Make Money.* 1870. Reprint. New York: Arno Press and the New York Times, 1971.

———. *Think and Act: A Series of Articles Pertaining to Men and Women, Work and Wages.* Philadelphia: Claxton, Remsen and Haffelfinger, 1869. Reprint. New York: Arno Press and the New York Times, 1971.

Phelps, H[enry]. P[itt]. *A Record of the Albany Stage.* Albany, N. Y.: Joseph McDonough, 1880.

Phillips, Catherine Coffin. *Portsmouth Plaza: The Cradle of San Francisco.* San Francisco: John Henry Nash, 1932.

Pickett, LaSalle Corbell. *Across My Path: Memories of People I Have Known.* New York: Brentano's, 1916.

Pitou, Augustus. *Masters of the Show As Seen in Retrospection by One Who Has Been Associated with the American Stage for Nearly Fifty Years.* New York: Neale Publishing Company, 1914.

Poggi, Jack. *Theatre in America: The Impact of Economic Forces 1870–1967.* Ithaca, N.Y.: Cornell University Press, 1968.

Quinn, Arthur Hobson. *A History of the American Drama: From the Beginning to the Civil War.* 2d ed. New York: Appleton-Century-Crofts, 1951.

Rabkin, Peggy A. *Fathers to Daughters: The Legal Foundations of Female Emancipation.* Westport, Conn.: Greenwood Press, 1980.

Rayne, Martha. *What Can a Woman Do: Her Position in the Business and Literary World.* Detroit: F. B. Dickerson, 1884.

Reignolds-Winslow, Catherine Mary. *Yesterdays with Actors.* Boston: Cupples and Company, 1887.

Roberts, Vera Mowry. "'Lady Managers' in Nineteenth-Century American Theatre." in Ron Engle and Tice Miller, eds. *The American Stage: Social and Economic Issues from the Colonial Period to the Present*. New York: Cambridge University Press, 1993.

Robinson, Alice M., Vera Mowry Roberts, and Milly S. Barranger, eds. *Notable Women in the American Theatre: A Biographical Dictionary*. New York: Greenwood Press, 1989.

Roorbach, O. A., Jr. *Actors As They Are: A Series of Sketches of the Most Eminent Performers Now on the Stage*. New York, 1856.

Rourke, Constance. *Troupers of the Gold Coast, or the Rise of Lotta Crabtree*. New York: Harcourt, Brace and Company, 1928.

Samples, Gordon. *Lust for Fame: The Stage Career of John Wilkes Booth*. Jefferson, N. C.: McFarland and Company, 1982.

Sanger, William. *History of Prostitution*. New York: Harper and Brothers, 1858.

Scott, Clement. *The Drama of Yesterday and To-day*. 2 vols. London: Macmillan and Company, 1899.

Sherman, Robert L. *Actors and Authors with Composers and Managers Who Helped Make Them Famous*. Chicago, 1951.

Sicherman, Barbara and Carol Hurd Green. *Notable American Women: The Modern Period: A Biographical Dictionary*. Cambridge: Belknap Press of Harvard University, 1980.

Skinner, Maud and Otis, eds. *One Man in His Time: The Adventures of H. Watkins Strolling Player 1845-1863*. Philadelphia: University of Pennsylvania Press, 1938.

Skinner, Otis. *Footlights and Spotlights; Recollections of My Life on the Stage*. Indianapolis: Bobbs-Merrill Company, 1924.

Smith-Rosenberg, Carroll. *Disorderly Conduct: Visions of Gender in Victorian America*. New York: Alfred A. Knopf, 1985.

Sothern, Edward H. *The Melancholy Tale of "Me."* London: Cassell and Company, 1917.

Stansell, Christine. *City of Women: Sex and Class in New York, 1789-1860*. Urbana: University of Illinois Press, Illini Book Edition, 1987.

Steele, Rowena Granice. *The Family Gem: Miscellaneous Stories*. Sacramento, Calif.: Old State University Steam Presses, 1858.

Stoddart, J. H. *Recollections of a Player*. New York: The Century Company, 1902.

Stone, Henry Dickinson. *Personal Recollections of the Drama*. Albany, N.Y., 1873. Reprint. New York: Benjamin Blom, 1969.

Strang, Lewis C. *Players and Plays of the Last Quarter Century*. Boston: L. C. Page and Company, 1902.

Towse, John Rankin. *Sixty Years of the Theatre, An Old Critic's Memories*. New York: Funk and Wagnalls Company, 1916.

Trollope, Mrs. [Frances] *Domestic Manners of the Americans.* Vol. 1. London: Whittaker, Treacher and Company, 1832.

Vandenhoff, George. *Leaves of an Actor's Note Book.* New York: D. Appleton and Company, 1860.

Vicinus, Martha, ed. *A Widening Sphere: Changing Roles of Victorian Women.* Bloomington: Indiana University Press, 1977.

Wallack, Lester. *Memories of Fifty Years.* New York: Charles Scribner's Sons, 1889.

Walsh, Mary Roth. *"Doctors Wanted: No Women Need Apply": Sexual Barriers in the Medical Profession 1835–1975.* New Haven: Yale University Press, 1977.

Watson, Margaret G. *Silver Theatre: Amusements of the Mining Frontier in Early Nevada 1850 to 1864.* Glendale, Calif.: Arthur H. Clark Company, 1964.

Welter, Barbara. *Dimity Convictions: The American Woman in the Nineteenth Century.* Athens: Ohio University Press, 1976.

———. *The Woman Question in American History.* Hinsdale, Ill.: Dryden Press, 1973.

Wemyss, Francis Courtney. *Twenty-Six Years in the Life of an Actor and Manager.* New York: Burgess, Stringer and Company, 1847.

———. *Wemyss' Chronology of the American Stage from 1752 to 1852.* New York: William Taylor and Company, 1852.

Whalon, Marion K. *Performing Arts Research: A Guide to Information Sources.* Detroit: Gale Research Company, 1976.

Willard, Frances E., and Mary A. Livermore, eds. *A Woman of the Century: Biography of Leading Women of America.* New York: Charles Wells Moulton, 1893. Reprint. Detroit: Gale Research Company, 1967.

Willard, George O. *History of the Providence Stage 1762–1891.* Providence: Rhode Island News Company, 1891.

Wilmeth, Don B. *The American Stage to World War I: A Guide to Information Sources.* Detroit: Gale Research Company, 1978.

Wilson, Arthur Herman. *A History of the Philadelphia Stage, 1835–1855.* Philadelphia: University of Pennsylvania Press, 1935. Reprint. New York: Greenwood Press, 1968.

Wilson, Garff. *A History of American Acting.* Bloomington: Indiana University Press, 1966.

Winter, William. *Brief Chronicles.* 1889. Reprint. New York: Burt Franklin, 1970.

———. *Life and Art of Joseph Jefferson.* New York: Macmillan and Co., 1894.

———. *Other Days.* New York: Moffat, Yard and Company, 1908.

———. *Vagrant Memories.* New York: George H. Doran Company, 1915.

———. *Brief Chronicles.* 1889. Reprint. New York: Burt Franklin, 1970.

Young, William C. *American Theatrical Arts: A Guide to Manuscripts and Special Collections in the United States and Canada.* Chicago: American Library Association, 1971.

―――. *Famous Actors and Actresses on the American Stage.* 2 vols. New York: R. R. Bowker Company, 1975.

PERIODICALS

Bank, Rosemarie K. "Louisa Lane Drew at the Arch Street Theatre: Repertory and Actor Training in Nineteenth Century Philadelphia." *Theatre Studies* 24-25 (1977–79): 37–46.

Berson, Misha. "The San Francisco Stage Part 1: From the Gold Rush to Golden Spike, 1849–1869." *San Francisco Performing Arts Library and Museum Journal* 2 (Fall 1989): 1–100.

Briscoe, Johnson. "The Mother of the Drews." *Green Book Magazine*, August 1912, 334–35.

"The Brooklyn Theatre Disaster." *New Yorker*, 26 April 1930, 35–39.

Bryant, Dolores Waldorf. "No. 77 Long Wharf: From Publishing Hall to Temple of Mirth." *California Historical Society Quarterly* 21 (March 1942): 75-79.

Davis, Tracy. "Actresses and Prostitutes in Victorian London," *Theatre Research International* 13 (Autumn 1988): 220–34.

Day, Charles H. "An Early Combination: A Summer Tour of Laura Keene and Her New York Company." *New York Dramatic Mirror*, 31 August 1901, 8.

Fife, Iline. "The Confederate Theatre in Georgia." *Georgia Review* 9 (Fall 1955): 305–15.

Galloway, R. Dean. "Merced Newspapers; A History 1862-64." 2 parts, *Acquisitions List Stanislaus State College Library* 6 (June and July 1967).

Harbin, Billy J. "Laura Keene at the Lincoln Assassination." *Educational Theatre Journal.* 18 (March 1966) :47–54.

Harwell, Richard B. "Civil War Theatre: The Richmond Stage." *Civil War History* 1 (September 1955): 295–304.

Hewitt, Barnard. "Mrs. John Wood and the Lost Art of Burlesque Acting." *Educational Theatre Journal* 13 (May 1961): 82-85.

Hipp, Edward Sothern. "Laura Keene's Death Scene Mystery." *Sunday Call* (Newark, N.J.) 10 February 1935.

Irvin, Eric. "Laura Keene and Edwin Booth in Australia." *Theatre Notebook* 23 (Spring 1969): 95–100.

Jenner, C. Lee. "The Duchess of Arch Street: An Overview of Mrs. John Drew's Managerial Career." *Performing Arts Resources* 13 (1988): 29–43.

Leiter, Samuel Louis. "Brooklyn as an American Theatre City." *Journal of Long Island History* 8 (Winter–Spring 1968): 1–11.

McDermott, Douglas. "Touring Patterns on California's Theatrical Frontier, 1849–1859." *Theatre Survey* 15 (May 1974): 18-28.

Marshall, Thomas Frederick. "Beyond New York: A Bibliography of the Nineteenth Century American Stage from the Atlantic to the Mississippi." *Theatre Research* 3 (1961): 208–17.

Morris, Clara. "The Dressing Room Reception Where I First Met Ellen Terry and Mrs. John Drew." *McClures* 22 (December 1903): 204–11.

Sherman, Susanne K. "Thomas Wade West, Theatrical Impressario, 1790–99." *William and Mary Quarterly*, 3d ser., 9 (January 1952): 10–28.

Stull, A. Frank. "Where Famous Actors Learned Their Art." *Lippincott's Monthly Magazine*, March 1905, 372–79.

Taylor, George Rogers. "Gaslight Foster: A New York 'Journeyman Journalist' at Mid-Century." *New York History* 58 (July 1977): 297–312.

Watson, Charles S. "Confederate Drama: The Plays of John Hill Hewitt and James Dabney McCabe." *Southern Literary Journal* 21 (Spring 1989): 100–112.

Welter, Barbara. "The Cult of True Womanhood 1820–1860." *American Quarterly* 18 (Summer 1966): 151–74.

Whytol, Russ. "An Entertaining Reminiscence." *New York Dramatic Mirror*, 25 May 1895.

DISSERTATIONS AND MASTER'S THESES

Barnes, Noreen Claire. " 'Actress of All Work': A Survey of the Performance Career of Louisa Lane Drew." Ph.D. diss., Tufts University, 1986.

Brooks, Mona Rebecca. "The Development of American Theatre Management Practices between 1830 and 1896." Ph.D. diss., Texas Tech University, 1981.

Cooley, Edna Hammer. "Women in American Theatre 1850–1870: A Study of Professional Equity." Ph.D. diss., University of Maryland 1986.

Creel, Richard Lowell. "The Effect of the Civil War on Nineteenth Century American Theatre." Master's thesis, California State University, Long Beach, 1973.

Deutsch, Helen Waverly. "Laura Keene's Theatre Management: Profile of a Profession in Transition." Ph.D. diss., Tufts University, 1992.

Duggar, Mary Morgan. "The Theatre in Mobile 1822–1860." Master's thesis, University of Alabama, 1941.

Faulkner, Seldon. "The New Memphis Theatre of Memphis, Tennessee, from 1859 to 1880." Ph.D. diss., University of Iowa, 1957.

Fletcher, Edward Garland. "Records and History of Theatrical Activity in Pittsburgh, Pennsylvania, from Their Beginnings to 1861." Ph.D. diss., Harvard University, 1931.

Hrkach, Jack. "Theatrical Activity and Other Popular Entertainment along the Turnpikes of New York State from the End of the American Revolution to the Beginning of the Civil War." Ph.D. diss., City University of New York, 1990.

Hume, Charles Vernard. "The Sacramento Theatre 1849–1885." Ph.D. diss., Stanford University, 1955.

Lawlor, Jo Ann. "History of the St. Charles Theatre of New Orleans, 1888–1899." Master's thesis, Louisiana State University, 1966.

Leiter, Samuel Louis. "The Legitimate Theatre in Brooklyn 1861-1898." Ph.D. diss., New York University, 1968.

McDavitt, Elaine Elizabeth. "A History of the Theatre in Detroit, Michigan, from Its Beginnings to 1862." Ph.D. diss., University of Michigan, 1946.

Manser, Ruth B. "The Influence of the American Actress on the Development of the American Theatre from 1835 to 1935." Ph.D. diss., New York University, 1938.

Morgan, Kathleen Anne. "Of Stars and Standards; Actress-Managers in New York and Philadelphia, 1850–1880." Ph.D. diss., University of Illinois, 1989.

Sherman, Susanne K. "Post-Revolutionary Theatre in Virginia." Master;s thesis, College of William and Mary, 1950.

Stolp, Dorothy E. "Mrs. John Drew, American Actress-Manager 1820–1897." Ph.D. diss , Louisiana State University, 1953.

Swain, James Walton. "Mrs. Alexander Drake: A Biographical Study." Ph.D. diss., Tulane University, 1970.

Taylor, Dorothy Jean. "Laura Keene in America, 1852–73." Ph.D. diss., Tulane University, 1966.

———. "Representative Women in the American Theatre during the Nineteenth Century." Master's thesis, University of Texas, 1950.

Weaver, Joan. "Sarah Crocker Conway: Actress-Manageress." Master's thesis, Indiana University, 1982.

Whitehead, Marjorie R. "Sarah Kirby Stark: California's Pioneer Actress-Manager." Master's thesis, California State University at Sacramento, 1972.

OTHER UNPUBLISHED WORKS

Barriskill, James M. "An Index to F. C. Wemyss' Twenty-six Years." In Billy Rose Theatre Collection, New York Public Library at Lincoln Center.

Durang, Charles. "The Philadelphia Stage, from the Year 1749 to the Year
    1855. Partly Compiled from the Papers of His Father, the Late John
    Durang, with notes by the Editors [of the Philadelphia *Sunday Dispatch*]"
    7 May 1854 to 8 July 1860. Microfilm copy, New York Public Library
    at Lincoln Center, of scrapbooks in the University of Pennsylvania library.

ARCHIVAL SOURCES

Billy Rose Theatre Collection, New York Public Library at Lincoln Center,
    clipping files, scrapbooks
Brooklyn College, Rare Books and Manuscripts, History of the Brooklyn
    Theatre, unpublished manuscript by T. Allston Brown
Brooklyn Public Library, local history files
Folger Shakespeare Library, letters to Augustin Daly (8 from Laura Keene, 1
    from Minnie Conway, 9 from Sarah Conway), 26 letters from Louisa Lane
    Drew to Daly and others
Free Library of Philadelphia, Theatre Collection, playbills, clipping files
Harvard Theatre Collection, Harvard College Library, clipping files
Library of Congress, Manuscript Division, Laura Keene papers
Maryland Historical Society, 2 letters from Laura Keene
Museum of the City of New York, Theatre Collection
New York Public Library, Research Libraries, Rare Books and Manuscripts
    Division, Olympic Theatre Account Book, 1864–65

Index

About the Author

JANE KATHLEEN CURRY is Assistant Professor of Theatre and Speech at Montana State University-Northern, Havre, Montana. A native of Moline, Illinois, she received a B.F.A. in Theatre from the University of Illinois, completed an M.A. at Brown University, and a Ph.D. in Theatre at the Graduate Center of the City University of New York. Her research interests include the nineteenth-century American stage and the participation of women in theatre throughout history.

ISBN 0-313-29141-1

9 780313 291418

HARDCOVER BAR CODE